LEAD
GENERATE

61 DAYS
TO DOUBLE
YOUR PAY

SCOTT GROVES

Lead Generate. 61 Days to Double Your Pay

Copyright © 2018 Scott Groves.

Book Design: Matías Baldanza, for Chasing Kites Publishing.

ISBN (ebook):

ISBN (paperback): 978-1-7325912-0-2

www.ConsolidatedCoaching.com

DEDICATION

Dedicated to my Wife, Karina, and my three children Gabriel, Alina, and Jonathan. You four have given me the inspiration, motivation, dedication, and space needed to complete this book. Thank you.

5 TIPS BEFORE YOU GET STARTED

Do these things right now to help ensure your success and commit to 61 Days of Lead Generation:

- Commit to reading a chapter a day as early in the day as possible. Right as you wake-up is ideal, before you start your work day is required. I know it sounds corny, but say it out loud or write it down five times in a journal. *"I will commit to lead generation for 61 days"*. Do it, even if it feels uncomfortable. It will help reinforce your commitment consciously and subconsciously.

- Set a calendar reminder right now, daily, for the next 61 days (calendar days or business day, you choose). Set it on both your personal and work calendars from 9:30 - 10:30 a.m. and title it *"Focused Lead Generation."* We can adjust this as we work through the book - but just put this recurring calendar reminder on the books right now. Invite anyone else you work closely with and/or anyone most likely to try to disturb you during this time.

- Follow me on Facebook for tips, ideas, videos on lead generation, and support at: www.facebook.com/MeetScottGroves

- Download the Audible app on your phone.

- Buy a book on audible that you can listen to over the next 61 days. I want you to simultaneously be working on your commitment to the *"system"* and *"habit"* of lead generation - that's what this book is for. However, I also want you to be improving your skills that relate to the actual sale, conversion, or relationship building techniques you will need once you are committed the lead generation activity.

CONTENTS

CONTENTS

CONTENTS

FOREWORD

The first time I met Scott, I was a newbie in the mortgage business. Having recently realized the career I went to grad school for was a mistake, I was recommended by a friend to become a loan officer. I had nothing else in mind at the time and he drove a fancy car, so I figured I would give it a try.

One of the company's onboarding requirements was a visit to its operations center in Tempe, AZ. I flew in the night before and stayed at a hotel. The next morning, all of the new hires were directed to meet in the lobby to be shuttled to the operations center. I remember walking out and instantly thinking I didn't belong. These loan officers were some of the best dressed people I had ever seen, wearing jackets, ties, shoes, and watches that easily added up to thousands of dollars. Then there was me—dressed in a wrinkled polo shirt and jeans.

Throughout my time in the business, I have learned that the typical sales introductions were already underway that first morning as each loan officer sized up the others, trying to one-up each other in product knowledge, sales volume, and stories about the *"good ol' days"* before the 2007 mortgage industry meltdown. I listened in silence (an invisible fly on the wall) and remained that way the entire shuttle ride.

FOREWORD

Once we arrived at the operations center, we were welcomed by the divisional sales manager. After some typical corporate mumbo jumbo, he let us know that we were in for a big treat. The company's number 1 loan officer in the country was also on location. He had just funded over $12 million in loans the previous month, and he was going to share with us a nugget or two of advice during lunch.

After completing the first half of the day's training, lunch began. Many people wandered in and out of the large conference room and were greeted by the loan officers. During this time, one person walked in unassumingly and sat in the corner of the room. Dressed in jeans and t-shirt, he was obviously one of the maintenance guys taking a break.

After some time passed, the divisional sales manager gave a brief intro and asked for Scott Groves, the number 1 lender in the company, to walk to the front of the room and share some of his wisdom. Applause started—then slowed with confusion as the unassuming person wearing jeans and a t-shirt began to walk to the front.

Scott, without speaking a word, had already taught the group of loan officers in fancy clothes a value greatly needed in all sales professions—humility.

The following day, I noticed many of the flashy loan officers dressed down a bit, and my fear of not belonging was eliminated.

This was just the first of many lessons I learned from Scott over the next few years. His openness that day made me feel comfortable enough to look him up in the company directory, and unsurprisingly, he took me up on my offer for coffee.

After I read a few books that he recommended at our initial coffee meeting, he could tell I was serious about my career choice. The rest is history, as he took me under his wing and began to coach me—with no financial incentive, I might add.

Scott's mentoring covered both life and business—lessons that led me to more than doubling my income from 2015 (when I got into the business) to 2016. After only two years in the mortgage industry, I bought my first house (no small feat as a single dude in Los Angeles), and I easily broke a six-figure income for the first time. Now, as I write this in early 2018, I had my best month ever during the *"slow"* time of year. All of this has happened in less than three years in the business, and before reaching the age of 30.

I take credit for pursuing the action necessary to achieve this level of success. However, I attribute much of what I have accomplished to Scott's mentorship. I see many colleagues, often with many more years' experience, making mistakes that I would be making if I was not fortunate enough to meet Scott early on.

In the following chapters, you will find many of the same nuggets of wisdom Scott has freely shared with me over the past few years through his coaching, mentoring, and friendship. While many top producers in sales hold their *"secret sauce"* close to their vest and won't share, Scott is an open book.

I am forever grateful for this top producer who had no financial incentive to help me, yet took the time to be my coach and share with me his lead generation tactics. I am certain you will share a similar type of gratitude should you invest the time and energy to read this book and implement the wisdom on its pages.

~Cole Strange, Loan Officer, Los Angeles California - May 2018

AN INTRODUCTION
WORTH READING!!!

In a Subway sandwich shop on May 13, 2008, I was grabbing dinner with my dad. Two $5 footlongs, the Subway Club of course, and two large drinks. Probably $14.87 worth of food at America's largest fast food chain. I was counting on Dad to grab for his wallet first when we reached the register. To my horror he said, *"Hey buddy, I left my wallet in the car. Can you get this one?"*

The moment had come. My chest tightened, and I silently swore at myself before speaking. *"No, Dad, I can't. I'm broke."* I set down my tray and walked out, too ashamed to look back. Tears welled up in my eyes as I walked towards my Corvette, a car I could barely afford to put gas in. My dad followed after me looking for some type of explanation.

For nearly eight years, I had been a busy loan officer in the richest state in the country. I funded more than a thousand home loans and home equity lines of credit at Washington Mutual, and I had earned nearly $1 million in salary, commissions, and bonuses. However, seeing the writing on the wall, I left WaMu 10 months before it failed and was taken over by Jamie Dimon at Chase Bank.

AN INTRODUCTION WORTH READING!!!

Unfortunately, the financial damage was already done by the time I jumped off the sinking ship. My 401K, which was largely invested in WaMU stock, was completely gone. I cashed out the remaining $17,000 right before the stock slid to below $10 a share, living off that money for a few months. I was suddenly an unemployed, non-college graduate, with a one-company resume, and desperately trying to find a job.

Beyond broke, I was sleeping on my friend's couch as I rented out my home to try and keep it from foreclosure. I had bought a house at the peak of the market and managed to wring a first, second, and third mortgage out of it. All the money from the mortgages was gone, and I was about $100,000 underwater. I couldn't sell it, so I rented it out. During this crisis, I married and divorced, gained weight, and took up poker to earn some spending cash (although I didn't always lose, it was not a good source of revenue that I could actually count on). I thought about bartending, dealing poker, underwater welding—anything to avoid dealing with a job in the financial markets again.

I took the last few thousand dollars I had in savings and spent it on attending a wedding in Belize for a friend of mine. I had basically resigned myself to some middle-management job at IKEA and declaring bankruptcy upon my return. I was close to $1 million in debt!

As it turns out, my trip to Belize ended up being full of good fortune—the birthplace of some lifelong friendships, and the beginning of some very important mentorships.

The groom was a successful Realtor as were several of the attendees. Kirk Gerou, the manager of a local real-estate firm here in Los Angeles was in attendance, and we hit it off. Kirk and I talked about the financial industry, the future of the housing market, and why an *"in-house"* loan officer position with Prudential Real Estate might make sense. *"Scott, lead generation and closing at least one deal a month is going to be key to your survival in the mortgage business,"* Kirk said on the flight back from Belize.

I applied for the job and started about a month later, just as my last dollar ran out. I had a small, guaranteed draw and about 60 days to start making some money. I learned about FHA loans and other loan products that were commonplace in the purchase markets. For most of my career at WaMu, I had only done refinances and second mortgages. I was ill-equipped to make the change, but I knew I could learn quickly and work hard.

I learned from experienced Realtors about the value of lead generation, prospecting, and staying top of mind with referral sources and clients. For two straight years I worked harder than anyone I knew. When I could afford to move back into my house, I found roommates who would exchange a few hours a week of busy work for discounted room and board. I started boxing to get back into shape and also to work off my anger and self-doubt. I began to pay off debt and regain my self-esteem. But the number one activity that changed my life was consistent lead generation. It's this skill, this habit, this business practice that I hope to instill in you over the next 61 days. Lead generation helped me redefine my life and definitely saved my career.

In time, I joined coaching programs and mastermind groups. I hired a sales and accountability coach. The father of an ex-girlfriend consistently gave me wise, honest counsel and became one of my most important mentors and advocates. As I put in the effort, my knowledge base and salesmanship improved, and I gradually developed lasting referral relationships with real estate agents who came to trust my ability to structure loans and close them. I moved companies twice before finding one with the culture and processes needed to serve customers, employees, and communities with honesty and efficiency.

Now, it's 2018. With good coaching, the right company, and hard work, I am (almost) debt-free, happily remarried, a father of three, an author (thanks for buying the book), and a coach for loan officers. I'm in better shape than I've been in years, and I am also generally at peace with the events of the past 2 decades.

I earned a high six-figure income last year and was a top 1% loan officer nationwide in 2014, 2015, 2016, and 2017. I work for a company I am proud of and have a sustainable base of referral partners. Most of this success has come from a commitment to do the daily lead-generation activities that generate referral relation-ships and focus on business success.

Lead generation has changed my life!

There will certainly be cycles in the real estate market, especially in Southern California, but I believe I will survive them thanks to consistent lead generation.

If you are lucky enough to have never hit rock bottom, be as-sured you needn't go there to succeed. In this book, I will teach you how to build the habit of successful lead generation in 2 short months—something that took me almost 15 years to accomplish. My goal is to help you double or triple your leads and your income over the next 61 days. Increasing the number of incoming leads by focusing on lead generation is the best tool we have to dramatical-ly improve our business, our income, and maybe even our lives.

You're about to embark on a 61-day Challenge that has the potential to transform your business, and possibly your life.

Unfortunately, it's very likely you will fail. Studies show that 82% of Americans do not stick to a budget for more than a month. It's been said that 92% percent of Americans abandon their New Year's resolution by year end with 50% quitting in the first month. Alarmingly, only 3-6% of Americans (depending on what study and criteria you review) are living a *"healthy lifestyle."* That means that without some help or accountability, 4 out of 5 people who start this challenge and read Day 1 won't be here on day 61. I want YOU to be one of the few who make it through this book, take the action steps required to lead generate, and make a real change in your business.

For additional resources & support, visit:
www.ConsolidatedCoaching.com/Resources

If you are in sales, you've seen these numbers before and they are worth committing to memory. They should also be a motivating factor and part of the reason why YOU commit to this process of lead generation for the next 61 days:

- 2% of sales are made on the 1st contact
- 3% of sales are made on the 2nd contact
- 5% of sales are made on the 3rd contact
- 10% of sales are made on the 4th contact
- 80% of sales are made between 5th and 12th contact

Conversely:

- 48% of sales professionals give up after the first contact
- 25% of sales professionals give up after the second contact
- 17% of sales professionals give up after the third and fourth contact

9

AN INTRODUCTION WORTH READING!!!

This means that 90% of salespeople give up before they get to the meat and potatoes of deal-making opportunities.

Imagine how much more successful you would be if you toughed it out and committed to being part of the 10% who didn't give up. What if you pushed through your fear and procrastination to ensure you were the 1 out of 10 salespeople who made that fifth, sixth, or seventh call required to close the deal or earn a new referral relationship?

This book, and the 61-Day Challenge within its pages, is about getting you into a lead-generation habit that will allow you to become one of the committed 10% who sticks with it, grows your pipeline, and dramatically changes your business and your life.

It's up to you whether you want to lead generate every single day, including weekends, for two straight months. Frankly, it's what I recommend. In almost any industry, we can find an opportunity to build relationships and talk about our product or service every day, even on Saturdays and Sundays.

If you have a family, strong weekend commitments, or are the type of person who needs weekend downtime to recharge your batteries, I understand. Working through this book on workdays, Monday through Friday, will still ensure that you have a three-month plan to get into a lead-generation routine.

This book is loosely arranged into sections, designed to move you along a strategic path that will give you the best chance of getting into a lead-generation rhythm. The concepts, while easy to understand, can be extremely difficult for many of us to implement. Therefore, the first week starts with some tactical action steps that will help set you up for success.

DAY 1

Find an Accountability Partner, Write a Check, and Commit Publicly

My best suggestion for making this program stick is to find an accountability partner, to shame yourself publicly, and to write a big check.

Step 1 – Find an accountability partner

TODAY, find someone who will hold you accountable. <u>Warning: your spouse, your best friend, your co-worker— these people will NOT hold you accountable for the next 60 days.</u> They know you too well. They know how hard you work. They will let you off the hook at any moment because of *"how much you have on your plate,"* and because they know that *"you already work so hard."* What you need is a hard-core acquaintance, a personal trainer, a coach, a manager who wants to see you succeed and knows just enough about your business to know that you can be doing more. Ask him to hold your feet to the fire for the next 61 days, even pay for this accountability service if needed. Just find someone, today, who is going to push you to be successful.

Step 2 – Let people know publicly that you are going to lead generate.

One hour a day—for the next 61 days. When you put this kind of goal out to the world, the world will help you complete it. That distant friend who loves to razz you on Facebook will post publicly to see if you're sticking to your announced goal. People at work and in social circles will be inspired, jealous, and curious about what you're doing. The conversations that organically occur because of your public proclamation can become lead-generating tools in and of themselves. Announce to as many people as possible what your specific goals are over the next 61 days.

Step 3 – Write a check.

Write it for just enough money that losing the amount written on the check would really hurt. For some it might be $50, for others $500. For me, I've found the magic number to be $2500. That's a lot of money—it won't bankrupt me, but it would really hurt to lose it. Now, make sure to write that check out to one of your competitors, a cause or political party you dislike, or a friend or family member who always borrows money but never pays it back. Address an envelope, attach a stamp, insert that check, and give it to your accountability partner with detailed instructions to mail the check if you don't complete the 61-Day Challenge.

I'm not saying you can never have a bad day. I'm not saying you have to be perfect. I am saying that you have to try every day, work harder if you miss a day, and GET to the END. We all screw up, it's going to happen. What defines success is being able to mess up or miss some key activities, and then get right back at it the next day.

If these three things don't give you enough motivation, peer pressure, and guilt you into committing to lead generating, then you seriously need to reconsider whether or not sales is the best career choice for you.

Now go spend 20 minutes doing the activities I just noted. Then go lead generate, whatever that means to you, for another 40 minutes.

Note to the reader:

Following several chapters throughout the book, I provide a question to help you implement each day's teaching. I don't claim to have all the answers. It would be arrogant and ignorant of me to assume that I know exactly how you can be successful in the arena of lead generation. What I do know is that I can help by asking good questions, adding my timely suggestions, and offering ideas that will help you clarify your vision and illuminate your path to success.

Who can you lean on, count on, and look to who will help you be successful throughout this journey?

DAY 2

Start a Spreadsheet – Track Your Leads and Referral Sources

Reality Check: What CRM (Customer Relationship Manager) do you use? It's unlikely you are using one efficiently, maybe even not at all. Maybe you have a corporate sponsored CRM that you *"kind of use."* Maybe you are like me and you've spent thousands of dollars over the course of your career on various CRMs, lead management systems, tracking software, and lead generation tools that never panned out.

If you're part of the 10% of sales professionals who truly use a CRM and have it fully integrated into your business life, then great—keep doing what you're doing. If you're like the rest of us, and I assume you are if you're reading this book, start a spread-sheet or Google sheet RIGHT NOW so that you can track your leads over the next 60 days.

SERIOUSLY, stop reading. Open your laptop and start a spreadsheet or Google Sheet right now.

DAY 2 – START A SPREADSHEET

Tracking prospects, knowing who your leads are, measuring your lead flow, and knowing which referral sources are actually sending you leads is pivotal over the next 60 days and throughout your career. It's also the second most powerful way, right behind lead generation itself, to grow your business.

All you need is 1 spreadsheet with 2 tabs and 6 columns under each tab.

The first tab on this spreadsheet is for incoming leads. The column titles should be: First Name, Last Name, Email Address, Phone Number, Referral Source, and Notes (for some professional/product context).

The second tab should be a list of EVERY referral source you ever encounter. (My list is currently up to 8,000 Realtors, title reps, escrow officers, accountants, financial planners, pool cleaners, co-workers, competitors, and professionals from various networking groups who have, or might one day, refer me a potential client.)

The column titles for the second tab should read: First Name, Last Name, Email Address, Phone Number, HOW YOU MET, and Notes Section (for personal information).

You MUST know where your leads come from. You must track every referral partner and lead, and you need to keep current contact information for each. If you don't accurately track your leads and consistently grow your database of referral sources, you will leave hundreds of thousands of dollars on the table.

At some point in the near future, the size of your database may become more important than the quality of your work. Let's try the following thought exercise:

You have done a lackluster job of databasing clients and referral sources over the last 15 years. You run your business in more of a reactive state versus a proactive state. You find yourself working more IN your business than ON your business. You never seem to 'get-to' those proactive lead generation and prospecting activities.

You can pull together 500 key names, phone numbers, and email addresses of people you work with, referral sources who know your name, and clients who have done business with you in the past. To be clear, you've done a GREAT job with these people! However, since you don't database very well, and hence you have not really nurtured this list of contacts, you've lost touch with a fair amount of these people. Additionally, you don't really even know how to contact the rest of the clients and referral sources you've interacted with over the years.

Conversely, let's assume that for the last 15 years I have been relentless about databasing any potential client or referral source I've come across. I currently have 15,000 names, phone numbers, and emails in my database (this is a real number, BTW).

What if tomorrow, a new product, service, or offering comes out that is going to be of interest to 2% of the people we both know. AND, let's assume clients in your database, since you are closer with them, are 5 times as likely to work with you as the people who are in my database (even though I've been reaching out once a month for years via Constant Contact and social media).

We both send out the exact same marketing piece to each of our databases.

> You have: 500 potential clients in your database x a 2% response rate = 10 lead/sale opportunities.

DAY 2 - START A SPREADSHEET

Let's say you close 100% of everyone who is interested. Remember, even though I'm nurturing with my database digitally, I'm not as close with my people as you are with yours. This probably means that my people are only one-fifth as likely to work with me as your people are with you.

> I have: 15,000 potential clients in my database x a 2% response rate = 300 lead/sale opportunities.

But remember, you're way closer with your people than I am with mine. You've probably done a better job, professionally, than I have. Therefore, I only get one-fifth of this group to buy from me. However, due to the size of my database, I still close on 60 sales opportunities versus your 10 sales opportunities. As you can see, the size of your database is monumentally important to the number of future sales that you can make.

So, what can you do today to start efficiently tracking leads and referral sources?

DAY 3

Clear Your Decks

I like to do my prospecting from 9:30-10:30 a.m. two days a week, and from 10:30-11:30 a.m. three days a week. My normal schedule goes something like this:

5:00 - Wake up, journal, plan my day, drink lots of liquids, check emergency emails.

6:00 - Workout.

7:30 - Breakfast with team, potential recruits, past clients, referral sources, or my family.

8:20 - Clear my Decks of any true emergencies. Quickly delegate any priority projects that absolutely cannot wait until 9:30.

9:30 - Start 1 hour of focused prospecting – OR – get through 25 contacts (whichever happens first).

10:30 (or whenever I'm done with 25 contacts) - Start my *"work day"* and focus on everything else.

Every other day, I push this entire schedule back one hour and spend that time in the morning working on my passion projects, like this book.

The key here is to clear my decks of any of those *"emergencies,"* (which frankly, probably aren't really emergencies) so that I can focus on the number one activity that is going to move the needle in my business and my life: lead generation.

Here are some ways that you can clear your schedule, remove distractions, and empower yourself to commit to lead generation.

1) **Go through your phone right now and do the following: Go to Settings > Notifications > turn ALL of them off other than text, calendar, and 1 or 2 others that are critical to your business, your life, and/or lead-generation activities.** The first time I did this I turned off *"auto-notifications"* on over 50 apps that were auto-pushing things to my phone and distracting me. We check our phones often enough that even your email *"push notification"* can probably be turned off.

2) **Learn how to set a DND—Do Not Disturb—function.** Turning this on for 1 hour a day when you do your lead-generation activity will ensure you don't get sidetracked by phone calls, emails, texts, or other notifications.

3) **Set an alarm for 15 minutes prior to when you plan to do your lead-generation activity.** Once that alarm goes off, clear your decks, hit the restroom, grab a tea or coffee, and let everyone around you know you are going into focused lead-generation activities for the next hour or so.

4) **Learn to INTERRUPT interruptions.** Tuning out distractions, staying focused, and telling people you are

working on a priority project are all skills that develop over time. For example, if you see a friend, client, family member, or manager calling you during your lead-gen hour, pick up the phone and simply say this:

"I answered the phone because of how important you are to me. Right now I'm in the middle of a very important hour of focused activity. Is this a matter that I can call you back on in about 60 minutes?"

It will feel uncomfortable at first, but it gets MUCH easier with practice. Respect your own time and schedule, and others will start to do the same.

Additionally, when I first adopted this technique, I was amazed to find how many incoming phone calls could be handled with a 30-second question, one sentence email, and/or could be handled by the person calling me once that individual knew I was engaged in my most important activity of the day.

How many digital interruptions can you temporarily or permanently turn off? How many ongoing interruptions can you pro-actively "interrupt"?

DAY 4

Do the Important Shit First

As I alluded to yesterday, for most salespeople, lead generation needs to happen first thing in the morning. The bottom line is that if you are a salesperson, entrepreneur, or fully-commissioned employee, there is nothing, and I mean NOTHING, more important than LEAD GENERATING.

The definition of lead generation—as Google Assistant dictated to me this morning—is the action or process of identifying or cultivating potential clients for a business product, service, or ongoing relationship. Until a prospect is identified, until a lead is obtained, until a sale is consummated via sourcing a client, NOTHING else matters. Your process, your conversion, your follow-up, your product, your service—NOTHING matters until you've generated a lead who can purchase, consume, or in some way build a relationship with you, your product, or your service.

With rare exception, I believe these lead-gen activities should take place in the morning roughly between 8:30-11:30 a.m. This is when you are most focused, fresh, and everyone else's problems have yet to become your problems.

DAY 4 - DO THE IMPORTANT SHIT FIRST

My experience has been that most people who don't want to lead generate in the morning are just procrastinating in hopes that something comes up throughout the day to give them an excuse not to do their prospecting.

> *What A.M. hours can you commit to*
> *focused lead-generating activities?*

DAY 5

Know Your "Why" and Visualize It

Companies (and individuals) need to know WHY they are doing what it is that they do. It's about going two layers deeper, past the 'what' you do and the 'how' you do it.

Simon Sinek's *Start With Why* or *The Golden Circle*

One of the secrets to staying committed to lead generation is all about knowing your Why. Every salesperson knows what they do. Some good salespeople know how they do what it is they do. The truly great salespeople, the ones who succeed at the highest level, know why they do it.

Spend the next 10 minutes, right now (prior to starting your lead generation), listing all the reasons why you do what you do. Why do YOU do it? Why does your COMPANY do it? Why do your clients, consumers, and business partners do what they do?

If you can understand the motivations, the inner spirit, the *why*, you will find it easier to stay motivated and committed on a daily basis.

Tying your daily activities to your why, to your dream, to your *"mission,"* can sustain you for a lifetime. Furthermore, connecting your why to the activity—to the result—can make you unstoppable.

What is the most important thing that will be most positively affected by you committing to 61 days of lead generation? Will you have extra money to send your child to summer camp? Will you get to pay off a debt? Take a vacation? Put an extra 3 months of emergency savings away for security? Help more clients experience your product or service? Donate more time and energy to a cause you're committed to? Get that promotion at work you've been striving for?

Whatever your one thing is, find a picture on the internet that represents that goal, that end result, that reason you are committed to lead generating. Make that picture your screensaver on your computer, the wallpaper on your phone, make it the background image of your life. Text it to your accountability partner and ask him to send it back to you once a day. Email it to me at Scott@ScottGrovesTeam.com and I'll send you the picture that drives my Why! Integrate that image of your success into your daily activity to help you stay motivated.

Now that you have your Why, you know your activity for the day that's going to move the needle (spoiler alert: it's lead generation), and you've found a picture that represents the outcomes of your success, you should be feeling a deeper commitment to your lead-generation activities and this book.

So, what is your picture—the actual physical picture—that represents your successful journey and outcome over the next 61 days?

DAY 6

Know That You're Going to Fail – And That's OK

Do you know how many rockets Elon Musk and SpaceX have exploded? By the time you read this book, it will probably be dozens. And I don't think he really cares. Elon realizes that each "failure" actually gets him one step closer to Mars.

We can look at lead generation the same way. Some days are going to be harder than others. Some days you're going to fail. Some days you're going to give up. Some days you're going to blow up your rocket ship and have to start over at the beginning.

The key is to reflect, resolve to do better, and commit to getting back to the lead-generating activities as soon as possible (preferably within an hour, but not longer than a day). This is where commitment OVERRIDES motivation. Motivation comes and goes, ebbs and flows. Commitment sticks!

Know now, as we are in the first week of this journey, that you are going to slip up. Don't let it distract you from the bigger goal of establishing a new habit, a habit that sticks. If you miss a day, commit to being better 24 hours later and get back at it. You can do it.

> *What could you accomplish daily, annually, in a lifetime if you weren't scared to try and you didn't let the small failures get you down?*

DAY 7

Get Uncomfortable

Have you ever worked out really hard? Like insanely hard? Right to the point of feeling you might puke or get injured?

Have you ever talked yourself into flirting with someone you really liked but who you thought might be out of your league? Sidenote: I have, and for reasons unbeknownst to me, she ended up marrying me. (We now have two beautiful children together.)

Have you ever tried something in business that everyone thought was crazy, and you made it work anyway? Good stuff, great stuff, amazing stuff happens when you go outside your comfort zone. It is during those uncomfortable moments that true growth occurs—when life starts to happen in really profound ways. <u>Get comfortable with being uncomfortable, and make your life happen.</u>

Ask any personal trainer, ask any business coach, ask any spouse, real growth happens when you're outside of your comfort zone. There is no growth in the safe zones of our lives. You KNOW this even if only subconsciously. Think of a time when you went outside your comfort zone. Maybe you had one too many drinks at a wedding and ended up dancing the night away. Even if dancing in public is the furthest thing from your comfort zone, having a little liquid courage made you do something you really enjoyed. Maybe in a moment of being fed up at work you did something or said something that was outside of your normal character, but it led to a great opportunity.

Now, think what might happen if you made more of these bold choices (without needing the influence of a few drinks), did things you naturally found uncomfortable, committed to something you normally wouldn't. Would it be crazy to think that you could dramatically and positively affect the course of your life if you made this a normal practice?

Nothing you are being asked to do throughout this book will hurt you. Nothing I'm asking of you will negatively affect your life. As a matter of fact, everything in this book is proven to make your life and your business thrive. Now is the time to get outside your comfort zone.

TODAY, call those referral sources, aged leads, or challenging clients who you KNOW you would never normally call. Get out of your comfort zone. It's never going to be as bad as you think. Usually, it ends up better than you could ever imagine.

Recently, I had to end a business relationship with a contract provider who was doing work for my coaching company, Consolidated Coaching, but who wasn't working out. The challenge was that I REALLY liked the guys I was effectively firing. I knew that they needed the money I was paying them and that the relationship they had with my coaching company was vital to their business's success. However, I also knew I couldn't keep paying them based on the value exchange of what I was receiving. It was a tough call that I put off for a month. Once I got out of my comfort zone and scheduled the call, I immediately felt better. And then, once I had the tough conversation and let the service provider go, I was genuinely amazed at how well it went.

We agreed to part as friends, to continue to work together in one specialized area, and to renew a scaled-down version of our business relationship in an area that was mutually beneficial for us both. It was truly one of those win-win scenarios.

My point is, even as I write this, I realize there are dozens of areas for growth where I need to step out of my own comfort zone. Let's tackle this together. Email me about one project, one client, or one referral source you are going to tackle today. I'll hold you accountable, and you can hold me accountable as I promise to respond with one thing I will do TODAY that is outside my comfort zone. Email me at Scott@ScottGrovesTeam.com.

What bold phone call can you make today that you would normally find way outside your comfort zone?

Congratulations! You made it through your first full week. We now know that you have the ability to commit to an activity and that you're possibly burning the candle at both ends as you grow your pipeline. However, most top producers in the areas of sales and lead generation tend to take a more holistic approach to their life, business, and health. So let's take a couple days to focus on the mind/body balance that will help improve additional areas of your life. All of this, of course, is to ensure we are taking care of the entire ecosystem that will help you with your lead-generation activities.

DAY 8A

Stay Healthy – Physically

Over the years, I've coached thousands of clients through a self-assessment exercise created to evaluate where you stand in different areas of your life. If you've ever been to a live personal development course, you've probably seen some version of the wheel below. I've seen it labeled in many different ways, some of which are trademarked, so I won't even try to give it a name here. Feel free to fill in the wheel, evaluating on a scale of 1 to 6 where you stand in your life.

For a more extensive self evaluation, visit
www.ConsolidatedCoaching.com/Resources

Almost as important as the *"wheel"* exercise itself, are the macro findings that I have discovered from leading large groups through this exercise. Whenever I poll an audience and ask the following question: which area of the wheel that you currently rated as *"poor"* has the largest impact on your ability to show up to work and lead generate on a consistent basis? The answer is almost always either Physical Health (about 75% of the time) or Mental Health (about 20% of the time).

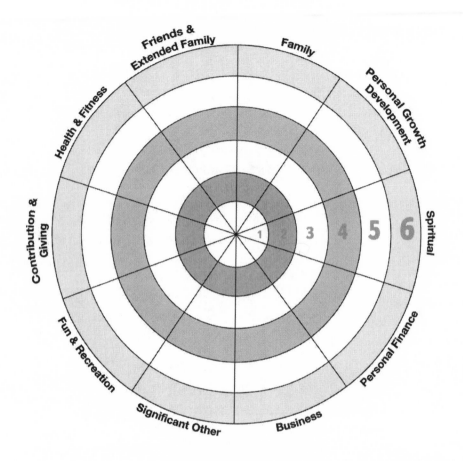

Wheel exercise

Apparently, salespeople have the ability to come to work, put their heads down, and lead generate when things aren't particularly good at home, with their finances, with their friends, and even with their community at large. But when a salesperson is feeling physically unfit and mentally drained (based on my non-scientific polling), it appears that lead generation activities go down by over 80%!

If your physical health isn't where you want it to be, if becoming a salesperson, business owner, or full time lead generator has caused you to pack on a few pounds, if you're not excited to be in your swimwear at your company's next top-producer event, then try these 5 tricks to kick-start your health:

1) **Identify one meal per day that is currently based on** *"bread"* **(sandwiches, burgers, burritos, tacos, pizza, etc) and exchange that meal for a healthy salad.** Stay away from fattening dressings and top off the salad with some healthy protein like salmon or chicken. Tell the waiter that you don't need the side of bread while you wait. Instead, drink some hot tea or green tea while you wait for your food to help further aid in digestion. This exchange of carbs for some leafy greens, protein, and a bit of caffeine from the tea will help you maintain your afternoon energy without the carbohydrate-induced sugar crash.

2) **Always take the stairs to your office (for as many flights as you can if you're in a high-rise).** Park in the farthest spot away from your office that will still allow you to walk comfortably inside. Replace moments of stress eating (we all have those moments in the sales business) with a brisk 10-minute walk around the block while you listen to a NON-business related podcast, guided meditation, or your favorite tunes, then take the steps back to your office!

3) **Sign up for a really nice gym.** A more expensive gym can force you to be more committed. Simply increasing the cost of your gym membership might be the recipe you were looking for to stay dedicated to your fitness. Try to avoid long contracts and try to pay per class so you can mix it up.

Personally, I belong to Equinox ($179/month), Hot 8 Yoga ($149/month), and I try to squeeze in 2-3 Soul-Cycle classes a month ($32/class). It may seem crazy to spend $500 a month on gym memberships, but is it any less crazy to spend that same amount of money on things that HURT your health? Try it! Add up what you spent last month on sodas, sugary coffee drinks, cigarettes, cigars, pizzas, alcoholic drinks with coworkers/friends/clients, candy, and fast food. I can almost guarantee that you spent at least $500 on items last month that are making you fatter, slower, and more prone to coronary heart disease. Why not shift that money to some fun, physical activities!

I heard a great quote from a health coach who teaches at my gym, *"If you don't make time for your health today, if you don't spend money on quality foods now, then you'll be forced to make time and spend money on your illnesses tomorrow."*

4) **Clean OUT the kitchen pantry.** My weaknesses are Oreos and Dr. Pepper... and pizza... and chocolate chip cookies... and sugary cereal. If I have any of these sugary/fattening items around, I'll for sure have a *"4th meal"* around 9:00 or 10:00 p.m., right before I go to bed. DO NOT fall into this trap. Get the junk out of your house. It will be an adjustment, but you and your loved ones will thank you after a few months.

5) **Do 1 hour of healthy activity per weekend that is out of your comfort zone.** That may be a simple 1 hour walk or hike. It might be a spin class, boxing class, or yoga class. If you are fortunate enough to live in a big city, almost every gym in your town will offer a free lesson, day pass, or week of free classes. Don't sign up and pay for 10 gyms, but rather take advantage of these test classes and try new things on your days off. It will change your life.

What 1 or 2 healthy habits can you adopt today to help you avoid the belly that frequently accompanies someone who is committed to lead generation?

Need help committing to your health goals? Download the app Telegram and find/message me, Scott Groves. I'll add you to our Consolidated Coaching health & wellness accountability group.

DAY 8B
Stay Healthy – Mentally

Start a daily practice of expressing gratitude, meditation, mental strength exercises, journaling, repeating affirmations, or whatever you want to call it. However you want to practice it, you need to take care of your mental health. Aside from yesterday's topic (physical health), the next best thing you can do for your body and your commitment to lead generation is to take care of your mental health.

Westerners appear to still be in the infant stages of understanding the power of focusing on our mental health. Even after seeing the scientific benefits of taking care of one's mental health, and the importance of developing a habit to show daily gratitude, I still find myself hesitant to adopt these practices as it all seems a little too hippie-dippy for me. However, I'm open to new ideas and figure I have nothing to lose. So, for the last year I've used a daily planner that helps me focus on reaching a positive mental state and ensures that I express gratitude for various things in my life on a daily basis.

DAY 8B - STAY HEALTHY - MENTALLY

My affirmation, which I write down daily, is as follows: I will spend less and save more so that I have the financial freedom to enjoy my family. I deserve to be, and will work toward being, disease free. I will focus daily on being a great man, leader, father, husband, coach, loan officer, manager, and citizen of the community.

I encourage you to try something similar. Everyday, right before you start your lead-generation activity, write out a positive affirmation and a list of three unique things you are grateful for.

My daily gratitude list has included items as obvious as my health, my children, my wife, and my job. However, this daily list has also included seemingly trivial things that make my life substantially better. Things like wifi, comfortable tennis shoes, sunscreen, enough income to pay for conveniences like Uber, eating out, and buying a new ergonomic computer mouse for my standing desk. I'm constantly working to find the joy and gratitude in the thousands of small things that fill my days and make this journey so much better.

Being in a good mental space is key to staying consistent with the daily grind of lead generation. Focusing on gratitude also affects other areas of our lives such as staying resilient, keeping to a schedule, and allowing ourselves to stay committed to challenging activities (like lead generation) without being beaten down by the emotions that come with frequent challenges and the inevitable *"No"* we get while prospecting.

Apps like *Headspace* can help us take this practice one step further. By carving out a specific amount of time every day, maybe start with 5 minutes, we can assure we are working on our mental skills at least as often as we work on our physical bodies, sales skills, and professional knowledge.

Find a way to focus on your mental well-being, and I promise you will see huge gains in all areas of your life including your health, relationships, business, and professional growth.

What is one daily practice of improving your mental health that you can commit to for 5 minutes a day? Have you tried Headspace™ or another similar app to meditate?

DAY 9

Time Block OR Activity Block – Don't Do BOTH

Time Blocking is dead. Okay, it's not dead, but it's probably on life support for those of us who generate most or all of our income via lead generation and sales.

I call it The Curse of the Amazon Generation. The reality is, there are few things I can think of that aren't currently available on demand. Most of the media I consume, the products I buy, and the services I'm interested in can all be ordered on demand for immediate delivery or within hours. Even something as intrinsically personal and vulnerable as dating has become as easy as 'swipe right' or 'swipe left.' This has created an environment where most referral sources and clients expect answers NOW.

I'll frequently step out of a long lunch appointment to see that a client or referral source has tried to reach me by call, text, voicemail, email, and sometimes Facebook Messenger or Instagram Direct Messaging. Recently, I lost out on a $2M refinance loan, a nice little commission, because I didn't realize my Facebook business page (not my personal page) had its own FB Messenger inbox. A couple of messages from past clients actually sat in that inbox for a few months before I discovered them. But I digress.

I point this out to illustrate that being available for our clients and referral sources must always be at the forefront of any schedule we attempt to design.

Instead of trying to time block, or schedule out our entire day (which I believe to be a less and less effective, practical solution for salespeople), I believe we should have a list of focused activities that we return to and try to do at some point during any given day.

Personally, I only time-block or schedule-out roughly 3 to 4 hours a day with non-negotiable items. These non-negotiable activities include my early morning workout (between 45 and 90 minutes daily), focused lead generation time that I commit to (30-60 minutes daily), and face-to-face scheduled appointments with my team, clients, referral sources, or recruits (roughly 60-90 minutes per day). That's it!

Even time with my family is fluid, ranging from full days off work where I'm totally detached from electronics to jam-packed workdays where I'm gone before my children wake up and I return home after they are asleep.

We could debate about scheduling and the merits of daily commitments for years. However, for the focus of this book, I want to talk specifically about that 30-60 minutes of daily lead generation that we all must commit to.

I want to be sure that you do NOT become emotionally attached to the outcome of these lead-generation activities, just do them. Results will follow! Schedule your daily lead generation time on your calendar, then commit to executing.

If you have started this journey by committing to 5 calls a day, you may find that the fear around making these calls can be paralyzing. However, once you overcome this fear through consistency of making the contacts, you can move on to calling 10 contacts a day, 20 contacts a day, and for some hard-core lead generators, 50 or even 100 contacts a day.

For example, in my mortgage business, instead of calendaring out every hour of every day, we commit to at least 30 minutes per day of lead-generation activity. We then supplement this daily block of time with *"themed days"* that further support our sales activities and production goals. For example, Marketing Mondays doesn't mean that we have set in stone to call 100 Realtors from 9:00-10:00 a.m. It means that in addition to our daily lead-generation practice, we commit a fair amount of time on Monday toward working on various marketing activities.

> *What are the three things you want to commit to daily that you can then build a fluid schedule around? SPOILER ALERT: one of them better be Lead Generation. Another one better relate to your health.*

DAY 10

Know Where Your Clients Come From

There is a reason why Day 2 of this book had you starting a Google Sheet or Spreadsheet. If you haven't yet done that—STOP what you're doing and DO IT NOW.

Remember my example on Day 2 about the size of my database versus your database? Recall that even if you are 5 times more likely to close a deal than me, the size of the database (in my example) netted me 6 times as many sales as you?

Obviously, the SIZE and quality of contact information in your database is the number 1 most important factor when it comes to using this data as a tool. However, a close second is being able to track WHO and from WHERE your leads are coming from. This, in-turn, allows you to evaluate the quality (and not just quantity) of your referral sources.

Do personal introductions convert better than online leads? Does Yelp create a more dedicated client than does Facebook traffic? Does John appear to be your number 1 referral source because he is referring you the most leads, but as it turns out, Jill is actually more valuable because she is converting a much higher percentage of her referrals into closed transactions?

These are the things you can only evaluate once you are tracking all your income leads and databasing all your referral sources.

Over the years, my referral partner Dan has become a good friend. We've enjoyed double dates, watching boxing matches together, and had lots of business lunches where we spent most of the time gossiping about other Realtors and laughing about tough transactions we had closed. At one point during 2015, I looked back on my lead tracking database and saw that halfway through the year, Dan had only given me about one-third the amount of leads he had provided me in the previous year. I still loved the guy, thought highly of him as a Realtor, and wanted to hang out socially. However, having quantifiable knowledge that his incoming leads had dropped off dramatically, versus going off the fact that I enjoyed conversations about business with Dan, allowed me to do the following:

1) Have a serious, fact-based conversation with Dan about why he might not be using me for all his business any longer.

2) Show Dan that I'm serious about my business, my tracking, my success, and the success of my business partners. This ensured a reinforcement of the business side of our relationship.

3) Bring something to Dan's attention that he was not yet willing to address and accept himself. His business had changed, it had shifted in a different direction that didn't include me, and some of it was drifting away from him completely.

4) Give myself peace of mind (again with facts, NOT anecdotal evidence) that I wasn't the problem. Dan's business had

slumped, and his ability to refer me new buyers at all was the real problem.

5) Decide how much more time I wanted to devote to this business relationship (while still being able to specify time to spend on our friendship).

Knowing WHERE your leads come from is key to continued business success and allocation of resources (time and money). It will also help you identify trends in your own business so you can strategize using facts and not emotions.

What benefits are you seeing from tracking your leads? What referred sources do you need to invest more or less resources into?

DAY 11

Commit Publicly – Write a Check – Burn the Ships on the Shore

If you've made it to Day 11, you're probably feeling good, maybe you've even seen some success in your lead-generating activities. However, 50 more days is a LONG WAY AWAY.

You need to write a check to someone or something you cannot imagine supporting. You have to publicly pronounce why you are writing that check and how this is going to motivate you to accomplish some kind of stretch goal over the next 50 days. Then you have to hand that check off to someone who you know will mail it.

Make the check out for an amount that's big enough to hurt.

I briefly mentioned this technique on Day 1, but maybe you weren't ready to commit back then or you needed to order some checks. Here's a peek into how I have successfully employed this strategy in my own life.

On April 1st of 2018, I wrote my friend and accountability partner, Simon Herrera, three checks:

- $1,000 check made out to the Donald Trump re-election campaign (a campaign I don't want to support).
- $1,000 check made out to the Clinton Foundation (a charity I don't want to support).
- $1,000 check made out to a competitor of mine who I am not fond of.

On April 30th of that month, the checks were to be mailed by Simon if I didn't accomplish the following goals:

- Finish this book.
- Weigh under 195 lbs.
- Generate at least 100 leads for our mortgage business.

I posted pictures of these checks in my coaching group on Facebook and on Instagram @ScottGrovesTeam (you can check it out for yourself).

Thankfully, I fully committed throughout the month of April, completed all three of these tasks, and got to burn all three of these checks over a celebratory cigar with Simon.

The idea here is to create some external motivation, an accountability system of financial penalties, and a physical representation (YES, write the actual physical check) that can help you commit to your goals.

Burn your ships on the shore (AKA, give yourself NO option to retreat or fail) and get to work on accomplishing those goals.

I did.

You can too.

Who are you writing this accountability check out to?

DAY 12
Know What Success Looks Like

Every industry is different; we all have our own metrics for success. But you want to know something funny? For most businesses it comes down to *"2 a day."* If you talk to, engage with, and build a relationship with 2 people a day, you will be wildly successful in your sales career.

Here is my underlying math.

I want to make $1,000,000 on a W2 selling loans, a goal I have yet to reach.

My average commission per loan is $5,000, which means I need to close 200 loans.

To close 200 loans, I need to get 250 loans into process (there is about a 20% fallout ratio in the SoCal housing market due to inspections, appraisals, cold feet on either side of the deal, failed negotiations, etc.).

To get 250 deals into escrow, I need about 500 pre-approved buyers.

DAY 12 - KNOW WHAT SUCCESS LOOKS LIKE

To get 500 pre-approved buyers, I need 750 at-bats, potential prospects, and/or quality leads who will commit to filling out a mortgage application.

Divide that by 360 days in a year — Yep, I have to talk to roughly 2 new people every single day who can become either clients or future referral sources.

Knowing what the path to success tangibly looks like—2 new connections daily—is so much easier to conceptualize than the generalized goal of *"I want to make $1,000,000."* When we know what a successful workday looks like, then we know what success looks like. That is how we become a success story in our business.

Just imagine what I could be capable of if I followed all the steps in this book, worked on my craft, lead generated for just one consistent hour every single day, and ended up generating four quality leads a day. I could probably double the size of my team, make closer to $1.5M, and work less by handing off more and more activities to my newly enhanced team.

> *How can you ensure that you are talking to two new leads or referral sources every single day?*
>
> *OR*
>
> *What DAILY metric do you need to be tracking to ensure enormous success?*

DAY 13

If You Don't Follow Up, They Won't Follow Through

One of my first paid coaches in the mortgage business, Todd Duncan, used to preach the following line over and over again:

> "If you don't follow up, they won't follow through."

This quote is extremely relevant in almost every industry. In the fall of 2017, I had ballooned to my highest weight ever, 224 lbs. For context, I wrestled in high school at a sturdy 152 lbs. When I got out of the Army, I was a fit 170 lbs. At times, in my 20s, when I was boxing and playing volleyball, I was an extremely fit 180. I used to laugh at guys (like my dad) who had let themselves cross over 200 or even 250 lbs. *"How can anybody get that fat,"* I would say to myself.

Needless to say, I found myself in this very same place as I approached 39 years old. I signed up for a very expensive gym in my area and attended my free one-on-one training session that came with my new membership.

The trainer I worked with during this complimentary session was insanely knowledgeable, very fit, and he had a good personality. It would have been easy for us to work together for months, and I looked forward to him holding me accountable as I was committed to my fitness goals. We left the complimentary session with a plan to talk within the week. He was going to send me some dietary supplement recommendations, and I was ready to drop $2,000 for 20 one-on-one sessions. Working together seemed like a foregone conclusion.

Then the unthinkable happened. He never followed up, so I never followed through. By the time he reached out 2 months later, I had already fallen in with a workout group from my office and didn't need his individual attention and accountability. I had found what I needed elsewhere, and this trainer lost out on $1,000 for himself and $1,000 for his company.

I highlight this story from my personal life as a reminder that even when the client is committed to us, and to themselves, we still need to follow-up. If not, we encounter the very real possibility of not closing the easiest of sales.

How can you consistently follow up with the clients and referral sources who you may have forgotten about? How about the ones who may have forgotten about you?

What CRM, spreadsheet, calendar reminder system, company work-flow, or external accountability system can you set-up so that you never lose a client again?

For me, I have three simple systems:

1) **Monday Morning Calendar Reminder** – This reminder, which pops up weekly at 8:30 a.m., has a running list of my key referral partners. I review this list every Monday to jog my memory about who I need to follow up with. This calendar reminder drives my Monday morning lead-generation activity.

2) **Google Sheet + Company CRM** – By tracking every lead I receive in a Google Sheet and adding every live deal to our company CRM, I ensure that I always have a digital record of clients I need to be engaging with.

3) **Company Post Closing Campaign** – Knowing that follow-through after the deal closes is the biggest item missing from my business model, I strategically aligned with a mortgage company who does all of this for me. Knowing my limitations, and handing off the portion of the follow-up activities that I know I'm bad at, has allowed me to focus more of my time on lead generating for new business.

Today, for 1 hour, reach out to those clients or referral sources on your list who are waiting for you to follow-up! Once you follow-up, they might just follow through.

Then, I want you to spend at least 30 additional minutes brainstorming about systems and practices relevant to your book of business that will help ensure you are consistently following up with top referral sources and clients.

What follow-up system do you need to implement right now?

DAY 14

Give Something Up

I run a coaching program that offers low cost, no strings attached, monthly coaching for loan officers. The value we provide via our trainings, live events, and archived material is INSANELY more valuable than the $59 per month that we charge. Considering that loan officers work on commission only, have no cap to their income, and can literally make an unlimited amount of money, it is SHOCKING to me how many loan officers won't invest in themselves.

I once posted the following to Facebook, in a group I run, that has over 2,000 engaged loan officers.

"Tell me you don't like my tie, tell me my content sucks, admit that you're just lazy...but do not tell me you can't afford $59 a month to invest in yourself. If anybody in this group can call me and tell me with a straight face that he or she doesn't spend at least $200 per month on cable, Starbucks, soda, and booze, I'll coach you for free."

To date, NOBODY has received free coaching. Two people tried, but once I reviewed their bank statement, they were both spending over $400 a month on DirecTV, booze, fast food, cigarettes, and Starbucks.

My point here is that life is all about making economic choices. What are you willing to give up in column A so you can get something out of column B. Here is another way to put it, what are you willing to STOP wasting your time on in order to make more money?

Follow my illustration below for how dramatically your time choices affect your income:

The TV Show Sons of Anarchy Cost Me $135,000.

There are 92 episodes in the TV show Sons of Anarchy—a great series my wife and I binge watched in 4 weeks back when we were dating. Each show runs about 44 minutes. 92 episodes x 44 minutes each episode = 4,048 minutes of TV consumed. Divide these 4,048 minutes of TV by 60 minutes in an hour = 67.5 hours.

If I stay truly focused and lead generate for an hour straight, I can generate a new lead (or a new referral relationship) that will turn into a closed deal within 12 months. My average commission per deal is roughly $4,000 before expenses, $2,000 after expenses and taxes.

At 67.5 hours x $2,000 per hour, that equals roughly $135,000 in revenue I missed out on by choosing a TV show over lead generation. Let's say I screwed around at work, got distracted, and only lead generated for 75%, 50%, or 25% of the time I wasted on this TV program. That's still $10,000, $33,000, maybe $67,000, that I left on the table.

Don't get me wrong, we all need downtime. That time spent connecting with my girlfriend may have been part of what led her to becoming my wife. However, in the digital age of endless distractions (which include the VERY addictive drugs of apps, TV, and social media), it's important that we evaluate how much money and business we are losing by the choices we make and how we choose to protect (or not protect) our time.

> *So, what activity is taking up your time and costing you money without you even knowing it? What are you willing to give up in order to make room to work on yourself, your business, and your lead generation?*

Congratulations, you've made it to the beginning of Week 3.

Some social and behavioral therapists would say you've made it over the first big hurdle. Most humans increase their ability to stick to a habit, task, or behavior after integrating it into their life for at least 2 weeks. Speaking from experience and having coached and managed hundreds of sales-people, I think that number is closer to 5 or 6 weeks. Whatever the number, we have a long way to go. However, I'm sure if you're lead generating at least 1 hour a day, you're already starting to see some results. If you aren't, that's OK. I had to meet, call, introduce myself, and reintroduce myself over 15 times to the referral source who ended up becoming my best source of business throughout 2015 and 2016.

I'm probably supposed to share something super inspirational here—something about your *"passion for lead generation"* or some other such nonsense. If you're reading this book, you prob-ably don't have a natural passion for lead generation. If we are being honest, you might not even have a passion for your job or career at-large. I'm here to tell you that's OK. Many of us, I would venture to say most of us, don't work in a job or career field we are *"passionate"* about. That doesn't mean you have an excuse to not work hard at it. You, like me, probably have reasons why you want to be as successful as possible and/or make as much money as possible. If you're going to be in a job that requires sales and lead generation then...

(answer on the next page)

DAY 15

Just Do It

Today, I'm just going to say: DO IT.

There is a reason Nike has made billions of dollars based on the simple slogan: *"Just Do It."* Al Sed, a friend and colleague of mine, has a great inspirational tale. At a conference I saw him tell a crowd of salespeople:

"Many of you are waiting for divine intervention to get the motivation to go do lead generation. It doesn't work that way. Commitment is the only thing that works! The universe, a higher power, The Secret, your spouse, your friends, they probably don't give a shit if you lead generate. No one is going to be uniquely interested in your ability or desire to lead generate until it's too late.

YOU have to want to lead generate as a way to better your life. You have to be committed to lead generation. Don't wait for motivation to kick in and just hope you'll do the activities—hope is not a plan. DO the activities, and that will create the momentum, the commitment, the inspiration, and the positive feedback loop you need in order to move forward and do the task of lead generation."

I find myself doing this when I take on new salespeople, come out of a coaching event, or make a public declaration about my lead-generating abilities. I find that these 3 activities force me to find my inner lead-generation spirit-animal and get to work. Many professionals don't need to learn a bunch of new stuff. However, we all have to be frequently reminded of stuff that we know we need to be doing right now!

Take 30 seconds to game plan, then just go do it. Don't wait for motivation to come, it won't. Build the momentum today by doing the activities and committing to what it is you set out to do.

What lead generation activity can you commit to "Just DO" today?

DAY 16

You Might Be Doing It Wrong, and That's OK

Yesterday, I told you to follow the advice of Nike's slogan and *"Just Do It."* Today, let's build on that concept with some of the ideas from Phil Knight's book Shoe Dog. Phil Knight, the founder of Nike, started the company with a few hundred dollars and a dream.

In the early days, he tried everything: mail orders, selling to friends, selling to coaches, selling to high school and college track athletes out of the back of his trunk at weekend track meets.

Frankly, Phil didn't know what he didn't know; he tried everything.

As the company began to grow, he flew to Japan to source manufacturers. Again, he tried everything. Talked to everyone. Toured any company or factory who would give him a shot.

My point here is that when it comes to lead generation, there is probably no *"wrong-way"* to attempt to get in touch with referral sources. Yes, throughout your career, at various times, and with various sources, you will find the "best" way to reach your target audience. However, if you're just starting to get into your lead-generation routine, it is unlikely that there is a "bad-way" by which to go about it.

Here is a partial list of ways I have tried to lead generate, market, and grow my personal brand:

- Direct mail
- Cold calling
- Warm calling
- Individual email
- Mass email
- Paid email campaign
- Facebook ads
- Facebook posts
- Facebook messages
- Myspace posts
- Mass texting
- Individual texts
- Flyers
- Yelp Ads
- Zillow ads
- Target marketing
- Google adwords
- SEO
- Group lunch and learns
- Happy Hours
- Individual meals
- Coffee appointments
- Educational seminars
- Informational webinars

- Newspaper ads
- Trade publication ads
- 3rd party software solutions
- Face-to-face office drop-ins

The funny thing is, and not too surprisingly, the 2 things I've had the most success with (even in this modern, techy world) are warm phone calls and face-to-face meetings.

Because no matter where our world leads us in terms of technology and convenience, I strongly believe that there will never be a true substitute for real, in-person relationships. Even with the reality that Google's new Artificial Intelligence will be setting appointments for us in the near future, I believe humans will still want the reassurance of other humans when it comes to big ticket sales processes like the purchase of a home, a car, or a business.

I could be wrong. Maybe in the future, lead generation and sales will all be handled by artificial intelligence, sales funnels, and bots. However, I still believe in the power of phone calls and face-to-face contact as a primary means of lead generation.

As a supplement, much like Phil Knight in the early days of Nike, I'm willing to try every angle possible to continue to lead generate and make sales.

So I ask you today, in what creative ways are you reaching out to your target audience in addition to your daily calls?

AND

In addition to your 5, 10, 20, or 50 calls a day, how else are you staying in front of clients and referral sources?

DAY 17

Invest in Someone Else

Nursing schools have a great motto and system for training: See One, Do One, Teach One.

The thought process behind the saying is that people learn the quickest, especially in fast-paced environments like an emergency room, if they:

1) Observe an expert performing a task.

2) Do the task.

3) Teach the task to the next person.

Even though you are only 2 weeks into your journey, those 2 weeks might put you light-years ahead of a coworker, friend, subordinate, manager, or recruit who cannot yet wrap his or her head around the power and importance of developing a daily habit of lead generation. Why not take this opportunity to bring on a mentee? You can improve yourself by practicing lead generation, by teaching someone else how to do it, and by holding someone who you want to invest in accountable to the activities.

Furthermore, from a growth standpoint, it is always good to foster deep business and personal relationships with 3 types of people:

1) **Someone older, wiser, and more successful than you (preferably someone who is working or has worked in your same profession).** Learning from a sage or mentor is how knowledge, life lessons, and practical experiences have been passed down for thousands of years.

2) **Someone on the same level as you, both personally and professionally.** I find building a competitive spirit, a sibling-rivalry with this individual creates the best type of accountability partner. It can also give you someone to (occasionally) commiserate with.

3) **Someone junior to you who is much less experienced in your craft.** Teaching and passing down your knowledge to a mentee can help remind you of the activities you should be doing and can strengthen your own skill set. Frankly, this time with mentees, has become one of the most rewarding activities I participant in weekly and monthly.

If you follow these three steps for successful learning—See One, Do One, Teach One—you surround yourself with the three types of people mentioned above. And you continue your commitment to lead generation. You may soon realize that the biggest gains in your business come from the steps in this chapter.

> *As you were reading this chapter, who came to mind as someone you want to learn from and someone you want to invest in? Set up lunch with these individuals!*

DAY 18

Know Your Guidelines and Your Craft

If you've ever attended a Tony Robbins event, you know that he warns you about something early on in the conference:

"Do NOT go home and preach to your friends and family about all the great stuff you learned! Don't comment on all the things they need to being doing differently in their lives, and don't share every tip and tactic you think you've mastered in the last 4 days!" Tony will say from the stage.

The truth is, everyone does it anyway. By natural design, we have an innate desire to share what we know. It's one of the ways we've survived as a species.

When you are knowledgeable in an area—just discovered a cool phone app, found the next great website, or are simply educating yourself on a specific topic—your inclination is to want to share that knowledge.

Although this can sometimes be an annoying habit, we need to embrace this instinct and use it in our business. When it comes to lead generation, sharing your knowledge is one of the most powerful tools in your tool box.

You see, when you know your craft, when you know your industry, when you understand the guidelines and technicalities of your product, that is when you have an unlimited amount of talking points to share with your prospects and potential referral sources.

When I hear salespeople say, *"I don't like to cold call (or warm call, or door knock, or host seminars, or call past clients) because I don't know what to talk about,"* what they are actually saying is, *"I'm not educated enough in my business to have anything interesting to say."*

When you have mastered your business, you will not run out of things to say. For example, coming out of the 2009 market crash as a loan officer, I was in bad shape. I made just over $18,000 that year. If I was going to survive, I had to start doing more low-money-down loans since nobody seemed to be able to scrape together a 20% down payment. The problem was that there was a competitor in my area who dominated the market and was an FHA loan expert (FHA loans being the leading product for low-money-down buyers). Instead of giving up and stopping my lead generation activity, I educated myself. I learned about every other low-money-down product, second mortgage product, and FHA alternative loan that existed in the marketplace.

For nearly all of 2010, I did 100% of my lead generation, cold calls, and warm calls talking to Realtors about FHA alternatives, and it served me well. By 2011, I made over $100,000 based on these efforts.

Industry knowledge, taking the time to learn about new products, and truly understanding my business gave me a strategic advantage over my competitors. It also created a shareable set of talking points that allowed me to create great marketing content and continue to commit to lead generation.

If you feel like there is a gap in your business or product knowledge, then today is the ONE day throughout our journey that I'm going to give you a pass on doing your lead-generation activities. Instead of lead generating today, focus one solid hour on learning something unique about your craft, your business, or the guidelines that govern the product you sell. Find the gap in your knowledge and fill it in. I guarantee you that this education will give you something to talk about with prospects and referral sources for weeks to come.

> *What are you going to learn today that you can work into your lead-generating calls?*

DAY 19

Themed Days—Marketing Monday

For the next 5 days, I will explain what my Monday through Friday looks like via the concept of *"Themed Days."*

As a loan officer, which has been my primary job for the bulk of my career, I find it VERY hard to time block. Other than the focused 1 hour a day I spend on lead generation (usually done from 9:30-10:30 a.m.), I find it difficult to stick to a daily agenda or schedule.

Disputes with clients, Realtors, and/or underwriters. Emergency pre-approvals. Deals that go into escrow randomly. Staffing issues. Marketing deadlines. All these things conspire against me and my ability to time block specific activities into specific hours.

What I have found effective are *"Themed Days."* By having a daily theme, I can focus on that theme throughout the day as free time and space appears on my calendar.

I call Mondays: *"Marketing Mondays."*

In addition to my hour-long lead-generation activities, Monday is my day to work on my personal branding and marketing.

I should probably define the difference between lead generation and marketing with a story that clearly explains the differences.

A loan officer friend of mine, Cole, who specializes in VA loans posted a very spur-of-the-moment Facebook Live video right as he was walking into an open house. The video was of him candidly explaining the importance of going to see listing agents to explain that receiving an offer to buy a house with a VA loan should NOT be problematic. He was talking about instilling confidence in the Realtor to feel comfortable accepting the offer, even though VA loans require no money down. Cole was marketing himself and combating the stereotype that buyers with no money down are somehow less qualified. They aren't less qualified, they are just taking advantage of their no-money-down VA benefit.

The video went viral, was picked up by a VA organization who reposted it, and ended up getting over 40,000 views and hundreds of likes and comments. This was branding. This was marketing. This was product awareness.

This marketing piece could have been repurposed into a sales flyer, email blast, Instagram photo, or dozens of other marketing campaigns.

Marketing is great, it's important. However, there is an important step, the lead generation step, that Cole missed. He should have individually messaged every person who engaged with the FB post saying something like, *"Hi, I'm Cole. I love doing VA loans. If you're ever in the market to buy or refinance using a VA loan, I would love to be your first call! Can I get your email to keep in touch?"* This would have been the lead generation side of the equation that so many sales professionals miss.

Marketing Monday has become the day when I write a blog post or create a video, which I then repurpose into an email blast via Constant Contact, LinkedIn post, Facebook post, and share to other online arenas.

I'll put up some live Facebook videos and map out my weekly social media strategy (if there is one). I send my weekly video email with product flyer to our top referral sources. I do all the 'marketing' tasks that set up my week's talking points which I address during my focused lead generation time.

> *What marketing activities could you accomplish every Monday if you dedicated yourself? What is the number 1 marketing activity you will commit to accomplishing this coming Monday?*

DAY 20

Taco Tuesday

Let's be clear, I don't always eat tacos on Tuesday. Even if I'd like to, it probably wouldn't be great for my diet.

Taco Tuesday is just a way of reminding myself to get belly-to-belly, break bread, and socialize with my referral sources so they don't drift away.

Tuesdays are the days where I try to schedule my group breakfast appointments, lunches, and/or happy hours with referral sources. I'll host a lunch and learn. Maybe take cookies and drinks to a bunch of open houses in my area (Realtors in Los Angeles preview their open houses for other Realtors every Tuesday from 11-1, and I found it to be a great time to get in front of dozen of agents). I'll do one-on-one dinners with my most important referral sources. I'll grab a 6:00 a.m. workout and a juice with some of my more active referral sources. Trust me, spinning, boxing, or doing Hot Yoga with a referral source will solidify that relationship like you wouldn't believe.

Overall, I use Tuesdays to double down on Monday's digital marketing activities with in-person meetings. I still try to make my 25 contacts during my Lead Generation hour. However, I also try to get face-to-face with at least 5, preferably upwards of 10, referral sources.

In some industries, based on geographical limitations, this might not be possible. Fine, try to get with at least one key referral partner every week on this day. Try new and creative ways, like an educational webinar, to get face-to-face with the people you count on for business. Even if these face-to-face meetings are digital in nature, I guarantee you it will help stay connected on a level that email and text simply cannot achieve.

I'm a huge fan of social media. The speed and efficiency of living in the digital world is great. But don't forget that nothing can replace the benefits of breaking bread with a referral source or client.

> *How can you design a day that allows for face-to-face meetings with new and existing referral sources?*

DAY 21

Work-Your-Ass-Off Wednesday

Sticking with my themed days of lead generation, I introduce you to Work-Your-Ass-Off Wednesday. I think there is a good chance my wife has never seen me on a Wednesday. This is a day where I abandon my family responsibilities, I spend hours working IN my business instead of ON my business. I play in the weeds, the dirt, focusing on the nuts-and-bolts of my business. However, I do not allow myself to abandon my lead-generation activities.

Wednesday is my day to work, hustle, catch-up, clear my decks of problem files, and double down on all things mortgage related. My schedule usually looks something like this:

4:45 - Wake up.

5:30 - Gym with 2-3 team members.

6:45 - Shower / Steam Room / Triage important emails by cell phone.

7:45 - Breakfast with as many people at my office as I can get to show up early for a free breakfast.

9:00 - Meet with possible recruits for a group interview.

9:30 - Office-wide pipeline meeting where every sales-person on our team (along with the support staff) does a deep dive into every active deal we are working on.

10:45 - Lead generation. I usually have a built-in list of referral sources, new and existing, to call from the discoveries made during the pipeline meeting.

Lunch - Usually with a recruit or referral partner.

1:30 - Catch up on email, respond to any inquiries my lead-generation activities have yielded, follow up with any clients or referral partners who may have interacted with social media posts and/or email blasts from Marketing Monday.

3:30 - Coffee appointments with new or existing referral partners who couldn't meet on Tuesday.

5:00 - Catch up on email, plan my Thursday and Friday schedules, and finalize personal plans for the weekend.

6:00 - Cigars, dinner, and coaching with top loan officers or team members.

8:00 - Write and/or play chess from cigar shop, often with team members or recruits.

10:00 - Home to a sleeping household.

I usually put in somewhere between 15 to 18 quality hours on Wednesday. I don't post this schedule to brag or insinuate that everyone has to be a workaholic. On the contrary, I feel like this one day of insanity allows me to be at peace when I come home early on other days of the week. By selecting one day where my family plans for my absence, I can commit to a hard-core day of lead generating with clients, recruits, and coaching my team on lead generation.

The success that comes from Work-Your-Ass-Off Wednesday allows me to be a better family man and free up time to pursue other personal goals. It also ensures I can take weekends off!

How could you design a day where you accomplish so much that it creates guilt-free time off?

DAY 22

Think-of-Yourself Thursdays

Thursdays are my slightly less hectic day. This is the day I think about myself and double down on managing my own mental and physical health.

I'll sleep in if my body tells me it's needed.

I'll spend some extra time at the gym in the sauna.

I'll follow my schedule a little bit less diligently.

I'll focus on giving and receiving coaching.

To be clear, I do still find an hour, usually in the early afternoon, to lead generate. I'll go through my lists of contacts who I have not been able to connect with during my normal morning lead generation times. The thought is that reaching out at a different time of day may increase my chances of making contact.

Knowing that my job frequently requires me to be engaged on the weekend, I will also use Thursday as my day to catch up on personal appointments, take a mental health break (AKA sneak out to the movies and have a Dr. Pepper), grab a yoga class, have lunch with a friend (who I may also try to turn into a future client), or just go for a long walk with the family.

It's while waiting for the movie to start, in a Yoga class, watching my kids play at the park, or on a long walk that I clear my mind and STOP worrying about loan files. It's also during these activities that I am creating space, which allows me to brainstorm additional techniques and motivations needed to grow my business.

Some of my best *"work"* ideas have come to me when work was the furthest thing from my mind.

For example, it was on a hike years ago that I recalled and important concept, from a seminar I had attended a decade earlier, about building relationships with listing agents throughout the escrow process. Recalling and expanding upon this idea while I hiked allowed me to create a follow-up plan that has put tens of thousands of dollars in my pocket over the last five years.

> *How can you create personal time where you think of yourself first, clear your mind, and allow new ideas to materialize?*

DAY 23
Follow-up Friday

If you plan to have a peaceful weekend, then you MUST eliminate the nuisance calls, the status update requests, and the *"request for more information"* that flood your inbox about deals already in process. You must close out the mental loops from work that are taxing your brain so you can recharge and enjoy your weekend!

There are very few fields where an accurate and immediate answer is needed on the weekend. If you want to avoid being pestered by calls, texts, and emails all weekend long, you MUST make a lot of status update calls on Friday. I call it Follow-up Friday.

I have mastered the art of giving Friday updates, and, non-update updates via phone. I update, by phone, all of my referral partners with whom I have an active deal in escrow. I also attempt to update all the clients who I currently have an active deal with. While delivering these updates, I'm conscious to use these calls as an additional lead-generation activity.

With each call, I deliver one very specific update and ask one very specific question.

First, I explain where the transaction has been (something like, the appraisal just came in at the contract price), then I let the client or referral source know where we are going (next, we have the underwriter sign off on the appraisal). If I know we are stalled, if we are waiting on something to move the transaction forward, I still deliver my 'no update update.' Something like, *"I have no new information to report, however, I wanted to call and let you know we are working quickly to resolve that problem we talked about earlier this week."*

Then I ask the question, *"On a scale of 1-5, how are we doing with our customer service and follow-through?"*

If I get a 1, 2, or 3, I obviously stop what I'm doing and ask additional, probing questions to try and fix the problem. My goal is to come up with solutions to move my service levels to at least 4 stars, preferably 5, and then I work that feedback into designing a better system.

If I get 4-star review, I ask for one specific item I can do better to move the service to a 5-star review.

If I get a 5-star review, I say thank you and that we plan to keep it up, and I ask for a referral. Normally my team carries a pipeline of roughly 15 active loans. Each deal has a potential referral source on each side of the transaction (a buyer's agent and a listing agent) and at least one buyer. This gives me 45 at-bats every Friday to try to get referrals.

Follow-up Fridays accomplish several goals. By delivering these updates I know this will free up my weekend. Additionally, it serves as a great opportunity to lead generate.

What Friday Follow-up could you enact to keep your clients and your referral sources informed? How could these updates create new referral opportunities?

DAY 24

It's Harder to Lead Generate When You're Broke

"The Rich Get Richer." It's a saying that, in the last 30 years, has gone from a rallying cry for success and hard work to a villainizing cry for social justice against high-wage earners.

There is a reason it's easier to make money when your financial house is in order.

When you have some savings and you're not fearful of where the next paycheck is coming from, your lead generation calls sound less frantic. When you know you have some savings to fall back on, lead generation is a skill to be mastered, an activity to be gamified. When you're broke, it's a means of survival, carrying an air of desperation into each sales call.

For the fully commissioned salesperson, I find that most financial problems boil down to one of two issues. You either have a revenue problem, or you have an expense problem. Lead generating, this book, and my coaching services (via Consolidated

Coaching—find out more at www.ConsolidatedCoaching.com) can absolutely fix your revenue problem.

I've personally been good (since the 6th grade) at finding ways to make money.

What I have personally NOT been good at is solving the ex-pense problem. I've overspent, under-saved, and invested poorly for most of my adult life.

Finally, around age 35, I found a formula that is starting to work for me. I HIGHLY recommend this system, or one like it, to anyone who works in the sales and commission field. Every dollar I earn gets split up as follows:

- 35% to taxes - A fixed tax rate comes out every paycheck: 27% to federal taxes and 8% to state taxes. This works for me based on my income, write-offs, deductions, and state where I live.

- 10% to savings, every paycheck, every time - I split this savings between IRAs, 401Ks, cash value life insurance, 529 plans for my kids, savings accounts, and mutual funds.

- 10% is reinvested into myself and my team - This bucket of money goes towards coaching received, belonging to mastermind groups, third party platforms I use, meals and entertainment with my team, investing in side businesses like Consolidated Coaching, and attending company retreats.

- 5% is donated to charity - This goes toward churches, charities or helping friends, and family in need.

- 50% to living expenses - Everything else. Rent, clothes, mortgage, food, cell phone bills, fun, travel, etc.

If you're playing along, you'll see I'm *"spending"* 110% of my earned income. This is ON PURPOSE. I constantly want to have organized stress in my life that forces me to push myself and work harder to earn more. If we ever head into another economic crash like we saw in 2009, I will probably cut my living expenses by 20%, cut my savings and charitable contributions in half, and double down on the coaching & personal development.

The reason for this is that a crash or disruption in our business cycle creates amazing opportunities to increase our market share. As others in our industry are washed out of the business, our lead-generation activities will keep us afloat. Then, during a recovery, those of us who remain in the game, thanks to our consistent efforts, will reap an overwhelming amount of the profits from the inevitable rebound.

> *What do you need to do between now and your next paycheck to ensure you are setting yourself up with the best possible financial situation? How would a more stable financial situation make you better at lead generation?*

DAY 25

Be InterestED, Not InterestING

Spoiler Alert: with rare exception, no one really cares what you have to say.

People want to be heard. There is a reason we have two ears and one mouth.

Do you want to know what separates good salespeople from truly exceptional salespeople? It's the ability to empathize and understand the referral source, prospect, or client by spending more time listening and asking better questions. Learn what drives your client, and then connect at the level where the client is interested in buying, NOT at the level of where you are interested in selling. This is where the magic happens.

Seek to underSTAND before you seek to be underSTOOD.

I've seen this time and time again with young salespeople who work for me. They are all fired up to teach the prospect, to educate, to show how smart they are. So they start a phone call or in-person meeting by regurgitating information, proving how smart they are by educating-to-death the person on the other side of the equation. They talk themselves out of a deal by proving how interestING they are.

You will be much better served by starting off, and staying, interestED in what the other person has to say. Actively listening will serve you well during your daily practice of lead generation. Ask good questions and then listen. This is in direct contrast to what most people do, which is to ask a question and then tune out while they wait for their turn to talk. Taking an interest in the life, successes, and challenges of the individual in front of you is one of the keys to success in sales and lead generation.

Focus your lead generation, sales process, and follow-up around the idea of being interestED, not interestING.

Questions like, *"Why does buying this product or service matter to you?"* is an infinitely better question than a sales script that tricks the client into saying yes. I highly recommend some additional reading on this topic and how it relates to sales such as Never Split the Difference by Chris Voss, and Conversations Worth Having by Starvos and Torres.

What 5-10 questions could you have ready to ask that will encourage you to go one level deeper during your lead-generation calls?

How can you change your sales script to include more questions and ensure you are interestED, not interestING?

DAY 26
Your Voice Is All You Need

I'm a big fan of handwritten notes, Constant Contact for email blasts, and other forms of written communication. At times in my career, I've used Facebook Messenger, MightyText, my company sponsored CRM, Instagram, and LinkedIn to get in touch with clients, existing referral sources, and potential referral sources. At times, I've even paid for *"professional marketing firms"* to take over this work for me.

There are two things I have learned from trying dozens of methods of communication strategies and platforms:

1) **With rare exception, you cannot afford the cost, the time, or the training it takes to create a *"substitute"* for your voice.** Your communication style, your writing style, your idiosyncrasies are your own. Consumers and referral sources have become too savvy, too educated, and too immune to the techniques of mass marketers. We can all tell when someone is sending us a form letter, a company sponsored marketing blast, or a cut and paste advertisement. Therefore, I believe in two of Gary Vaynerchuk's maxims—CREATE your

own content and MARKETERS ruin everything. Whatever you send out, be sure it's in your *"voice."*

2) **NOTHING works better than a phone call with your voice on the other end of the line.** There is no substitute for the sound of a friendly voice, a familiar voice, a voice that can instill confidence. Even a voice that is only heard via voicemail can be more powerful than dozens of other communication apps I've tried.

We all have lazy days where we want to hide behind email, Facebook Messenger, or social media blasts. However, please keep in mind that if you spend too many days mistaking marketing activities for lead-generation activities, your pipeline and your income will dramatically suffer over the next 90 days.

We must constantly be working on the following ideals as we make our sales calls:

1) Adding enough value and creating great content so that people will want to pick up our calls and return our messages.

2) Making those calls in hopes of having quality conversations or leaving great messages.

3) Having a plan to engage the client or referral sources who is gracious enough to spend their time on a call or meeting in person.

So today, think through your plan, know what you want to talk about, pick up the phone, get at it, and make 25 calls to new and existing referral partners.

DAY 27

Your Email Is Out of Control

If you've been doing all the right lead-generating activities for the past 3 weeks, then your inbox and voicemail is filling up quickly.

If email management wasn't already a big problem for you, get ready, it's going to be. Inevitably, sales professionals BACK-OFF of lead-generation activity right as momentum starts to kick in. We begin to mistake activity for productivity and say to ourselves (consciously or subconsciously), *"Email is full, leads are coming in, I can back off of the lead-generation activity."*

I get it! As of the day I'm writing this chapter, I went back to count my emails from yesterday. Between emails coming to me for my loan origination business, my coaching business, and my management responsibilities, I had 362 incoming emails to attend to. Add another 23 emails to that total from my personal email. It can become overwhelming. And, guess what, if you do the activities in this book, it's only going to escalate.

(Side note: find a tool like www.Unroll.me to help clean out your email of all unwanted subscription emails and advertisements.)

DAY 27 - YOUR EMAIL IS OUT OF CONTROL

You must get your email under control by practicing the 4 D's (or as I prefer, the 3 D's and 1 C) of inbox, voicemail, and task management.

DELETE – Is the message truly important? If not, get rid of it right now.

DO IT – If you come across an email, voicemail, or task, that can be done quickly, as soon you see it, then just do it and close out that loop. My rule of thumb is anything than can be accomplished in under 30 seconds should just be done at that moment in time.

DELEGATE IT – If the task can be delegated to someone with more bandwidth OR less earning potential than you, then hand it off and calendar yourself a reminder to check on completion.

In some coaching systems, there are 4 D's. The 4th D being "*defer.*" I don't like the idea of deferring as it seems too ambiguous, it gives my coaching clients an easy out to procrastinate, and has allowed me personally to back-burner very important correspondences.

I prefer swapping out the 4th "*D*" for another component which I call:

CALENDAR IT – In your calendar, cut and paste the body of the email you are concerned about, and set a calendar reminder to work on and complete the item at some future date. Invite any collaborators you will need to handle this email. I also add it to my daily written planner at some point in the future to check on completion.

After you do your lead generation today, spend an hour practicing the 3D's and 1C to get through your inbox quickly. Once you look at every email and voicemail through the lense of the 3D's &

1C, you will be amazed how quickly you can get through a task that may have previously taken up your entire day.

You can also use this system when you reach a point in your career where an assistant is helping with your email.

Your assistant can *"Do It"*, *"Delegate It"* as you or your representative, *"Delete It"*—which is probably the most powerful and will take the most training— and can calendar or leave for you to review.

DAY 28

Database an Office, Sector, or Target-Rich Demographic

When I was building my mortgage business and client list in 2002, my ex-girlfriend, our sisters, and I had a Saturday night routine. We would order pizza, get a case of beer, rent a movie from Blockbuster, and spend the night stuffing flyers and databasing. We spent about 4-8 hours every weekend collecting names and addresses of possible mortgage clients, databasing them, and then sending each person a promotional flyer for a Home Equity Line of Credit.

In 2009, after the market crashed, I adopted a different routine. Every deal I closed was precious. That year, I made $18,000, closing 8 or 9 mortgage transactions. Each time I closed a deal, I would go to the office website of the Realtors involved in the transaction and database every agent in that office. I would then call, email, and/or visit every Realtor in that office to let them know I had just successfully closed a transaction with Mr. or Ms. Realtor right down the hall.

This practice went on for about 5 years until I had 8,000 Realtors in my database who I could email, 2,000 agents as *"friends"* on social media, and 500 referral sources in a private Facebook group where I communicate with them about mortgage-related issues.

In the age of social media, LinkedIn, and every company putting up tons of information on their website, there is no excuse to not spend at least one hour a week databasing new, potential referral sources. You can go one step further by *"friend requesting"* potential clients or referral lead sources on Facebook, LinkedIn, and/or other social platforms. It's possible to *"get to know"* someone before you ever reach out to them for the initial meeting. On Instagram, my son's tag is #GabeTheBabe. I'm shocked when I call on a new Realtor and she mentions, before we have even met, how cute Gabe the Babe is.

Leverage these databasing tools to grow your network. As we've discussed, in the near future, the amount of money you earn will be HIGHLY determined by the size of your database.

What office, company, social group, or professional entity do you need to database this week?

DAY 29

You Are the Average of the Five People You Spend the Most Time With

Did you start this journey of lead generation with a friend, co-worker, or part of a coaching group? Almost a month in, are there people around you who are still committed to this journey, to lead generating, and to growing their business? If so, SURROUND yourself with more of these kinds of people.

Studies have shown, and I believe it was Jim Rohn who first pointed out, you ARE, or will BECOME, the average of the 5 people who you spend the most time with.

Think about it for a minute. Your 5 closest friends (or the 5 people you spend the most time with) probably make roughly the same amount of money as you. You are all probably in similar physical shape. You all probably enjoy the same activities socially. If your friends are hard-charging party animals who drink a fair amount and eat late-night fast food after leaving the happy hour that went too long, then you're probably carrying around a few extra pounds. Conversely, if you hang out with active people who enjoy the gym and the outdoors, you're probably in relatively good shape for your age.

If your closest buddies and family members are content to work a $55,000 a year salaried job, then your income probably reflects that. However, if you're surrounded by entrepreneurial go-getters who have no cap on their income, then there is a good chance you are making more money than you ever thought possible.

If you hang out with a bunch of self-centered materialists, then you're most likely very worried about and/or overspending on the car you drive. Yet, if you hang out with community-oriented friends who give back through church, community, or volunteerism, then there is a good chance you've done something altruistic in the last 30 days.

My point is that it's very hard to sustain the daily motivation to lead generate on your own. If you're around people who make excuses about never having time for lead generation, you will find yourself making the same excuses. If, however, you SURROUND yourself with 3-5 people who are hungry to do better in their careers, to affect more lives, and who want to make more money, you will find the tribe keeps you motivated. If you curate your friends and relationships carefully, I guarantee you the energy will be infectious.

At one point in 2014, after I had become the number 1 producer at a large, nationwide mortgage company, I did two things to ensure I was constantly working to level-up my game:

1) I started a volunteer check-in group with 10 top producers from around the nation who used to get on a weekly 30-minute call and exchange ideas.

2) I spent $10,000 of my own money to join a mastermind group with top producers from various industries.

By improving the circle of people I worked closely with, I increased my income by 45% from 2014 to 2015.

If you want to stay committed to lead generation, continue to surround yourself with other successful people, and upgrade your circle!

Who do you need to spend more time with, and who do you need to spend less time with, in order to reach your goals?

DAY 30

Reach Out and Touch Someone

In 2015, I closed 4 deals with a Realtor named Heather D. In 2016, I closed zero deals with her.

It wasn't until I did my 2017 business plan and looked back on my transactions from the previous two years that I realized I had completely lost touch with this referral source. It turns out that in that same year, Heather had dyed her hair, married, and changed her last name (which caused the Facebook algorithm to stop showing her in my feed). She also changed companies, which meant my emails were going to the wrong address. With everything going on in my career in 2016, I had literally lost track of this important, up-and-coming referral source who was at a pivotal point in her own career. I should have been doubling down on building that relationship, not letting it drift away.

Technology makes it easier and easier to *"touch"* people, stay connected, and ensure relationships like this don't drift away. In his book, The Millionaire Real Estate Agent, Gary Keller recommends you *"touch"* potential clients and prospects at least 33 times per year. Holidays, birthdays, milestones, market updates etc.

DAY 30 – REACH OUT AND TOUCH SOMEONE

I have some thoughts on this that I've fleshed out over the last 18 years of working on leads:

1) If you are in the business of trying to convert new online leads, cold traffic, or even leads that come to you by warm introduction; I believe you have to touch these leads two times a day until you move them to the next step of your process, or are told to go away.

2) In a competitive, high-volume, high-distraction business like the mortgage industry, you must *"touch"* your top referral sources once a week! This must be done either in person or by a telephone call. Even if you just leave a voicemail to check in and say Hi, then follow-up with a text message or email, you must do it.

   If you are out of sight, you are out of mind. In our fast-paced world, you might be shocked by how quickly you can fall off someone's radar and be replaced by another salesperson, product, or service. You should also be *"touching"* your top referral sources digitally at least once every week via email, facebook, instagram, etc. I use the *"follow first"* feature on Facebook to ensure that the activity of my top referral sources are constantly working their way into my social media feeds.

3) Clients who are *"pre-approved"* need to be touched at least once a month. Past clients, closed deals, and even clients whose deals have died off need to be touched by a phone call, in-person event, or at the very least a personalized email once per quarter.

As you increase your lead-generation activities and your volume of leads increases, you must ensure you keep in touch with past leads, the referral sources who presented the lead opportunities, and past clients. Without this constant touch, you run the risk of having to start over with new relationships every few months. Without systematic follow-up and a high touch system, it will begin to feel like Groundhog Day.

Today, in addition to lead generating for 1 hour, spend an ADDITIONAL hour scheduling your follow-up activity and brainstorming about unique ways to stay in touch with clients and referral partners. Demo a program like Contactually if you are looking for a digital solution to this problem.

In your business, how often do you need to "touch" key referral partners, past clients, and new leads?

DAY 31

Schedule and Attend an Event WAY out of Your Comfort Zone

Thanks to *Meetup.com* and other local affiliation groups such as *The Chamber of Commerce*, *Young Professionals Network (YPN)*, *LeTip*, *Business Network International (BNI)*, and *Rotary Club*, there are endless opportunities to attend a live event in your area. Find and schedule attendance at one of these events today. Right now! Find one and commit to going.

I know how you're feeling. Not only are you rolling your eyes as you read this, but you're also thinking, *"Why would I go to an event with a bunch of people not doing business, who want to socialize with other people not doing business? And those who are doing business already have their relationships established."*

Am I right? Are you frustrated with me for suggesting you go to one of these events?

GO ANYWAY! But go with a plan. Most of us go to these events, rush in at the last minute, talk to the people we know, have no purpose, and then leave disappointed. We walk out thinking the event was a waste of time. However, I would argue that we frequently have this feeling only because we didn't prep for the event.

Find out in advance who organized the event. Who are the key players in the group you should get to know? Can you get a list of attendees to add to your database? Are there second level connections you're trying to make with potential referral partners who know attendees of the event? Is there one key relationship you could establish that would make it worth going?

These are the kinds of questions you should ask yourself before you attend an event so you can make the most (and get the most) out of it. Lots of successful people generate a majority of their business from these get-togethers. Equally as important, professionals who attend these events with a plan generally add 10-30 professionals to their database after every event.

Today, I'm giving you a pass on your one hour of lead generation IF you commit to scheduling attendance at two live events. Find two different group functions to attend. Database the potential attendees. Do some recon on the event, the structure, and the player(s) you want to meet. Commit NOW to attending and making the most out of it.

| *What is one event you can attend this week?*

DAY 32

Tell Everyone What It Is You Do

I know a loan officer named John who is the absolute best at tactfully letting everyone know what he does for a living. His dental hygienist, his barista, his friends, family members, past co-workers from a previous career, everyone in his hiking group, and seemingly every acquaintance of his that we come across all know that he does loans for a living.

John has an uncanny ability to work a conversation about mortgages, real-estate, or the financial markets into every social setting. Without being pushy, he talks about his successes in the mortgage industry, he gives out cards, he gets a card from everyone he talks to, and he knows how to quickly build a personal relationship that may one day lead to a business transaction.

Similarly, in a digital fashion, and at the recommendation of my coach, I contact all 4,000 of my Facebook friends with the following message at least twice a year:

"Sometimes I forget to reach out and remind my friends, both in person and online, that my team is really exceptional at mortgages. When you, a friend, or a colleague are ready to buy,

sell, or refinance a home anywhere in America, I would like you to remember me as a free resource for reviewing your financials. Give me a call with any mortgage questions."

I do this with no judgment, no filter, and no reservations about the fact that I have to self-promote my business. The truth is, no one else is going to do it for me.

Whether you're more comfortable reaching out digitally, or in a personal setting, there is a way to ensure that your sphere of friends, family, and acquaintances KNOW what you do for a living, that you want to help, and that you are available as a resource.

> *How can you commit to connecting with your personal sphere and people you come across in everyday life? How can you tactfully talk about your business in a way that may create some lead-generation activities?*

DAY 33

Rinse, Repeat, Then Repeat Again, Again, and Once Again

You're over a month into your journey.

If you haven't given up yet, then I believe that you're going to make it to Day 61 and beyond. Remember, this is a 61-Day kick-start program, not a closed-end program. The goal is for you to develop a lead generation habit that carries with you throughout your career.

Chances are you've had a few failures and a few successes; you've lost motivations and then been spurred back into action. Or maybe you wrote that $1,000 check I mentioned on Day 11, and you just cannot imagine sending it!

Regardless of how you made it to this stage, take a moment to celebrate. Realize that in life, just showing up to the game constitutes about 80% of the effort that it takes to be successful. If you've committed to this first month of activity, then studies show that this lead generation thing is developing into an unbreakable habit.

DAY 33 - RINSE, REPEAT, THEN REPEAT AGAIN...

But here's the secret: this part of the journey in your business, this 1 hour a day of focused lead generation, it's NEVER going to change. The secret is that it is kind of like Groundhog Day. The names on your list might change. Your product might change. The medium by which you connect with clients might change. However, if you want to be successful, the activity of lead generating is never going away. And that's actually GREAT!

You see, you don't have to recreate the wheel. You don't have to worry, like many do, about guessing at how to be successful in your job. You don't have to agonize over decisions that could dramatically affect your business, your income, or your life. All you have to do is put in the time, commit to the activity over and over again, and lead generate.

I know it's not particularly easy, but it is SIMPLE. Today, in honor of Groundhog Day, rinse – repeat – and do it again. Spend an hour today lead generating, invigorated by the fact that you are liberated from the challenge of making tough, daily business decisions, and that you know your lead generation efforts will allow you to create the business and the life that you want.

Do you have the guts to target the people who have said "NO" in the past? Can you pick up the phone and call them again today to try to turn a no into a yes? How can you ask good questions to build a deeper relationship so that a no today turns into a yes tomorrow?

DAY 34

Know, Like, and Trust

You've heard this all before in some version or another. From the Bureau of Made up Statistics, it goes something like this, *"Most salespeople give up on the third call. However, did you know it takes between 5 and 12 contacts before someone says yes?"*

For me this wasn't much of a realization. As a loan officer, it was kind of a no-brainer to understand that dealing with the biggest financial transaction of somebody's life (or career), requires me to put in the work and make multiple contacts. I have to get my referral sources, and then their clients, to engage with me enough that I can move them up the ladder of knowing me, liking me, and then trusting me to handle their mortgage.

I don't care what the surveys or the statistics say. The bottom line is that we have to contact referral sources (and potential clients) as many times as it takes to move them up the relationship levels of *"Know, Like, and Trust."*

Does the referral source or client know who we are and that our name is associated with the product or service we are trying to sell? Does the referral source or client *"like"* us enough based on our presentation, our reputation, our lead-generation activities, or our marketing to give us a shot at that first relationship-building deal? And last, but not least, did we do a good enough job on the first deal and communicate often enough to earn their *"trust"* to get follow-up deals?

I don't care if you're a master salesperson who has read all the books, gone to all the seminars, knows all the scripts, and only takes one call to close a deal. I don't care if you feel like you cannot sell to save your life. No matter your skillset, you have to call the referral source or potential client enough times to move yourself up the scale of *"Know, Like, and Trust!"*

Today, in addition to your lead-generation activities, ask yourself which of these three areas you need to improve in business. Do you need more referrals to:

A) Know who you are and what you do?

B) Like you enough to give you a shot at that ever-so-important first deal?

C) Trust you and your systems enough to give you follow-up and repeat business?

If you need help in these areas, email me at scott@scottgrovesteam.com

DAY 35

Can You Bat .400?

Since 1941, when the science of pitching began to take root, no baseball player has ever batted over .400. That means that the best athletes in the world, men who train their entire lives to master the technique of hitting a baseball and get paid millions of dollars to do it, cannot successfully connect with the ball to get on base any more than 3 out of 10 times. Put another way, a world class player is someone who strikes out, flies out, or grounds out nearly 7 out of every 10 times he is at-bat.

If a player could decrease that number to only *"failing"* 6 out of 10 times—he would literally be the best baseball player of all time. Think about this, seriously think about it for a moment. The difference between a .250 batting average (getting on base 25 out of 100 times at-bat) versus a .350 batting average (getting on base 35 out of 100 times) is the difference between a hall-of-famer making millions of dollars a year, and a minor-leaguer not even making enough money to pay the rent.

Luckily, I'm not asking you to measure your wins in such minute increments. All I'm asking you to do is just pick up the phone, lead generate, connect as often as possible, and practice. Take the swings and get the at-bats. Connecting with the ball will come. If you spend an hour a day lead generating, you may only connect with the ball one out of twenty times. However, that's one more connection you would not have had if you had not taken the swings at all.

Eventually, you'll start *"hitting"* more frequently, connecting with more line drives, doubles, and even some home runs.

Keep this in mind the next time you lead generate. Are 3 -4 out of 10 people you call picking up? Are you talking to 3 or 4 people every time you do an hour of lead generation? If so, then you're batting at nearly hall-of-fame level. Talking to 5, 6, 7, or more people per hour is where you literally start playing a different game than most of the competition.

Don't get discouraged by the swings that result in a miss. You should only be afraid of the swings you never take.

Are you giving yourself enough at-bats
to become a "Hall-of-Fame" hitter?

DAY 36

Are You a Shotgun or a Sniper Rifle?

Two of the loan officers I respect the most, Justin (my business partner) and Daniel (one of my fiercest competitors who I hope to work with one day) are sniper rifles. I'm a shotgun.

Let me explain what I mean. Justin and Daniel have built their (VERY) successful careers "one shot at a time." One deal, one relationship, and one on-time or early closing at a time. They have both been precise, specific, and strategic in their approach toward referral partners, clients, and even the programs they allow into their portfolios of product offerings.

Slow and steady wins the race when using this approach. Both Justin and Daniel kill the competition by being silent assassins who *"take down"* relationships one at a time. Minimal marketing, minimal social media exposure, and more of an introverted approach has created great opportunity for both Daniel and Justin. They never waste their time by mistaking mass *"marketing"* for the important, one-off lead-generating activities that they know will actually lead to business and put money in their pockets right now. Dangerously, they are probably missing several at-bats with potential referral partners because, in a way, they've kept their expertise a secret.

I, on the other hand, tend to kick down the door as I light up the room with shotguns blasts (metaphorically speaking of course). Throughout my career, I have talked to every referral source, big and small. I've spent way more than my fair share of time on social media marketing and building brand recognition. I've tried out almost every platform, marketing tool, networking strategy, and every other digital, shiny object you can think of.

Like Justin and Daniel, I've also built a very successful career, just in a different way. The downside is that this strategy can turn off a lot of introverted, top-producing referral sources. And, when I make a mistake, everyone hears about it from the referral sources who may feel betrayed that my follow-up was not as good as my initial impression. The upside is that brand recognition and staying top-of-mind gets me at-bats on a lot of deals that would have naturally gone to other loan officers.

Technically, there is no "wrong" way to build your business as long as you do it honestly. However, I suspect that the future of sales will see top producers merging these two styles. The key is to be self-aware and know how you operate. Don't try to be someone you're not.

If you prefer to go extremely deep with a handful of referral sources by connecting with them more often than is standard in your industry, then great. You do you. Just don't forget that there is value in putting yourself out there to a larger network of referral sources. Try to do at least one thing a month that is outside your comfort zone, which puts you in the path of 5-20 referral sources who you may have otherwise not had an opportunity to get in front of.

If you want to be more of a public figure, spend your time marketing and attracting leads and referral sources on social media, then great. Again, you do you. Just don't forget to merge all those marketing activities with lead-generation activities. For example, if you want to spend your time producing a great video or piece of content for social media, no problem. HOWEVER, make sure you do the follow-up by messaging those who interact with your content, adding them to your master database, and following up with them for actual business opportunities as often as is appropriate.

Now, go spend an hour lead generating and perfecting either your sniper fire or shotgun blasts.

Are you more of a sniper rifle or shotgun? How can you balance one approach with the other?

DAY 37

Shiny Object Syndrome

If yesterday you decided you want to adopt the sniper rifle approach of lead generation versus the shotgun approach, I commend you.

Truth is, going back 20 years to Basic Combat Training in the Army, I've never been that great at zeroing in on one target. In the Army, when you first get your rifle, you go through a process called *"zeroing."* The process is pretty simple: shoot a small target from a short distance away, group 3 shots very close together, then adjust your rifle sights to ensure those three shots are hitting the target in the center. My drill sergeant back at Fort Benning was frankly worried about me being an infantryman. He could not, for the life of him (or me) figure out why 2 of my 3 shots were always spot on, yet 1 was always way off target. I guess even then I couldn't focus on one task for long.

If you're planning on the sniper approach of lead generation, this means you pick off and secure one relationship at a time, you go super deep with a small group of referral sources, and you tie your income to the success of a smaller-than-average pool of referral sources and clients. With this approach, you can never allow yourself to suffer from SOS: Shiny Object Syndrome.

Shiny Object Syndrome, a mainstay of the lead-generator who takes a shotgun approach, will wreck a sniper's career. You have to be laser-focused on the task at hand and the clients in your pipeline, and you must close every deal smoothly. If you're like my partner, Justin, who gets almost all of his referrals from five key partners, losing one source of business could drop your income by 20-25%. Lose 2 key relationships and you are headed for tough times.

Keeping track of your referral sources' business successes, while also keeping an eye on any personal challenges they may have that could affect their productivity, will be key to your own success. Treating every single referral from these core partners as your golden egg is necessary. Mastering open communication and Fierce Conversations (great book, by the way) is going to be critical to your success.

Do NOT allow yourself to get Shiny Object Syndrome and lose deals or relationships that your style of business does not allow for. If you find yourself losing focus on a relationship, client, or process, clear your decks and schedule a one-on-one call with that party. Reconnect as quickly as possible.

> *How will you know if you're getting off track with one of your key referral sources? How can you ignore and block out shiny objects?*

DAY 38

Don't Get Analysis Paralysis

If two days ago you decided that your lead-generation style is more in line with the shotgun approach, great. I'm the man who can personally coach you to a successful career via lead generating. Email me at scott@scottgrovesteam.com.

The truth is that this book is MY attempt to cure my own deficiencies. I seek to avoid Shiny Object Syndrome and merge my marketing tasks and brand awareness into daily lead-generation activities. This should allow me to put more deals in my pipeline by staying focused.

As I mentioned yesterday, Shiny Object Syndrome is a mainstay of being a shotgun marketer. It's a blessing and a curse. The reality is that we will waste a lot of time trying out new marketing ideas, strategies, and tools that never work. We tend to be early adopters. So when we do find something that works, it delivers in a big way, and we look smart for finding the new *"it"* tool. However, when a project doesn't work, we may find ourselves, or our team, upset about the time invested and ultimately wasted on the failed project.

For example, my business partner and my team can probably discuss, in great detail, the 10 platforms that have ended up as failures. I'm sure they aren't happy about it. However, a recent grand slam has been the use of BombBomb (signup at www. BombBomb.com/ConsolidatedCoaching). BombBomb, a video email & messaging platform, has helped our team and our clients standout in a BIG WAY. We closed dozens of transactions in 2018 thanks to the early adoption of this platform.

By video messaging the listing agents on properties that our buyers are making offers on, we have seen our client acceptance rates increase dramatically. In my business, getting referrals is good, and putting together pre-approvals for qualified borrowers is gold; however, it's not until we have a buyer under contract (or in escrow) that we actually have an opportunity to close that piece of business and make money. I work in the very competitive Southern California marketplace. Properties for sale often average 10 offers. By increasing our clients' acceptance rate by 20% through the use of video, our team has put tens of thousands of dollars in our own pockets, while also helping more clients get what they want.

However, as a shotgun shooter, we have an additional layer of risk in our business (due to our personality type) other than just wasting time on shiny objects. It's also possible that we can load ourselves up with so much work, so many ideas, new tactics, strategies, and options that we end up getting AP—Analysis Paralysis. AP is a condition in which someone has so many options, so many things they can take action on, and so many ways to contact leads and referral sources that they actually just sit there, stare at their computer, and do nothing.

If you've ever suffered from AP, I have the cure to kick-start you back into activity. It's called: THE PHONE. Pick it up, and with no fear, judgment, or reservation, CALL the top 20 people you've done business with or want to do business with.

This will reset your hardware, get you working again, and get your mind off the 5, 10 or 20 projects you want to work on.

> *Are you suffering from Analysis Paralysis? The solution is probably the smartphone that currently resides in your pocket or on your desk.*

DAY 39

If Possible, Prospect in Your Own Backyard

At a gym I used to attend, there was a very attractive young lady who worked out every day at the same time as me. I am a happily married man, so I never had an excuse to chat with this young lady without it feeling like some type of inappropriate flirtation. One weekend, as my wife and I hiked the Echo Mountain trail up the street from my work, we ran into this lady and her husband.

Having seen each other dozens of times at the gym made it easy to strike up a conversation on the trail as we were both with our spouses. We made some informal introductions over a water break and trail mix, talked about the gym, and became friends. Eight months later, I wrote a $600,000 loan for this couple. This kind of opportunity does NOT happen unless you do some amount of lead generation and prospecting in your neighborhood. Life is just easier if you're prospecting in your own backyard.

These at-bats (the ones that only occur when you work and live locally) are one of the major reasons I have a hard time hiring sales professionals who have to drive too far to get to work, or to a home base of operations.

Maybe you have heard of the parable, Acres of Diamonds. A miner (or farmer depending on which variation of the story you've heard) sells his *"worthless"* mine (or farm) to go prospecting for diamonds (or gold, or oil, or some other expensive commodity) far away in foreign lands. The buyer of his mine toils away and eventually strikes it rich right there on the property that used to be owned by the man now searching for riches off in a distant land. The seller, who traveled far and wide to strike it rich, sadly, dies poor and lonely.

Trust me, I understand the allure of working on the "other side" of town (or the state, or the country, or the world). For example, Realtors from all over Southern California hang their license at various Beverly Hills brokerages in order for their business card to have the coveted 90210 zip code. They hope that just having this address, without actually being part of the community, will help them obtain a multi-million-dollar listing. The reality is, most of these agents would probably do just as well (if not better) by becoming local area experts in their own neighborhoods and farm in their own backyard.

There is so much value in running into referral sources and clients at the local Starbucks. Interacting in the community with a referral source who you are trying to court is the best way to build rapport—try to serve the local community and build relationships where you are instead of trespassing on richer soil. This approach of organically connecting in your local neighborhood is a great supplement to your daily lead-generation strategy.

> *What "acres of diamonds" are you missing out on in your own backyard?*

DAY 40
Lead, Learn, and Coach

On Day 24 I told you to start getting a budget together. If you're like me, and not great at managing your finances, go back and read that chapter.

One of the things I suggested was to spend 10% of your income on your education, personal development, business growth strategies, and investing in your team. As of Q2 2018, I'm projected to make about $600,000 this year. Finding ways to invest 10% of my income back into me, my business, and my team is getting harder and harder, yet also MORE and MORE important.

As I level-up in my career, and start to zero in on exactly which top-producing referral sources I want to align with, there appears to be only two ways to break through to the top 1% of profession-als I want to work with. My personal "mission" has to align with theirs, (something I may or may not be able to do) OR I must have a skill I can educate them on. I have to bring value above and beyond the "transaction." I have to be able to coach or add value in additional ways.

DAY 40 - LEAD, LEARN, AND COACH

My friend and Coaching partner, Mike, has done this beautifully. Mike parlayed his investment in himself into a physical product, a book. Mike will openly admit that his book, Closer Than You Think, has only sold around 1,000 copies. He wrote the book after attending several personal development seminars and business conferences. Far more important than the book itself, however, is that Mike has created amazing talking points that allow him to approach top-producers with whom he wants to work.

He has used this book as a tool to start conversation, offer something tangible to leave behind for top producers to review, and Mike can now offer to come teach principles from the book to the team and support staff of these top producers.

Now, I don't expect you to rush out and write a book. I can tell you from experience that it's harder than you think (if you're thinking about it though, I highly recommend you google Chandler Bolt and check out his SPS courses). However, what you can do is take something you've learned in this book, something you've recently learned at a trade conference or seminar, or some piece of compelling training that is from outside your industry or product offering, and then teach it (with no obligations) to potential referral sources.

If you work in a business-to-business (B2B) type of setting, buy 10 copies of this book (email me for a discount at Scott@ScottGrovesTeam.com). You can teach a course to your refer-ral sources and business partners on how they can more effectively lead generate for their own business.

Whatever your angle is, take your personal and professional development seriously. Find something to teach. Be a coach to others. Share a message and see how dramatically that can affect your relationship with existing and potential referral sources.

Now, spend 20 minutes reviewing, recapping, and organizing your thoughts around something you've learned from this book or a recent sales conference. Go make 20 calls right now to referral sources who may be interested in learning more about this topic.

What is the one thing you feel most comfortable teaching to other business professionals or referral sources?

How can you leverage this to get in front of top professionals in your industry?

DAY 41

Count on Your Team

If you are a fully commissioned salesperson and count on lead generation for your livelihood, then chances are you have some type of support staff helping you out. In almost every job or business endeavor, you have a team.

Never, ever, take this team for granted. Yes, you are presumably the rainmaker. You bring in the deals. You create the relationship, the at-bats, and the revenue stream that keeps everyone fed. If your job is to lead generate, you probably also have the ability to make more money than anyone else on your team.

However, don't lose sight of the fact that you are frequently able to close deals, retain clients, build new relationships, and attract new referral partners because of the team's hard work that goes on behind the scenes.

In the mortgage space, depending on the level of your production, you may have a loan officer assistant, production assistant, pipeline manager, processor, underwriter, closer, junior loan officer, and/or a myriad of other positions, all created to support you in spending more time lead generating and structuring deals. One of the first questions I ask prospective coaching clients in the interview process is, *"Who is on your team?"* It infuriates me when I hear answers like *"I don't have a team."* Or *"It's just me."* Or *"I haven't hired anyone yet."* BULLSHIT! If you don't treat the other people at your company who help you close and retain business as a part of your team, you are missing a huge point of leverage.

Treat your team members well and then lean on them to help you accomplish your goal. Hold them accountable without micromanaging them. Read a book or two on management and delegation (I highly recommend starting with *The One Minute Manager* by Ken Blanchard and *Extreme Ownership* by Jocko Willink). Lean on the resources you have so you can spend more time working ON your business instead of IN your business. Spending more time on lead generating and less time on administrative tasks will ensure you take your pipeline, your business, and your life to the next level.

> *Who are the people at your company that you need to start looking at as part of your team? How can you consistently honor your team so they support you in your lead-generation activities?*

DAY 42

Model Success

Quick, name the person at your company who is the absolute BEST at what YOU do? Who are the top 5 people at your company who also do what you do? Stumped? Already number 1 at your company? Are you the only lead generator at your company? Quick, name the person in your industry or field who is the BEST at what you do.

Today you are going to lead generate NOT for business, not for referral sources, but for people who can become potential mentors, mastermind partners, and/or career advocates.

Success leaves clues. From every top producer, senior employee, and even a competitor, you can take away one small piece of wisdom (maybe even a big piece) about how you want to model your success. Success leaves clues, and it's up to you to find them. Analyze what other professionals in your space are doing to be successful and figure out what works for you.

Chances are there is a top producer, manager, senior associate, or colleague at your company who would be all too happy to talk about themselves. Contrary to popular belief, top producers also find ways to build relationships with their top competitors. Even cold calling a top producer can be flattering enough that he or she will take you up on a free lunch to talk about themselves.

Today, I want you to take a break from generating leads and instead generate ideas and relationships. Set at least 4 lunch or coffee appointments with people in your field who are doing it better than you are. Call your manager, senior person at your company, top producer in your field, colleagues, and maybe even competitors. Let them know that you've been following their ideas, emails, newsletters, production reports, or coffee room conversations for a while now. Let them know you're almost two months into a lead-generation coaching program. Offer to send a copy of the book to him or her for free with the hope of getting their top 2-3 tips on lead generation, business development, and/or relationship building over lunch (which you'll pay for of course).

At worst, you'll make some valuable connections and ensure that the top producers in your field know your name. At best, you'll find a highly valuable resource and mentor. With some quality conversation you can update your own game plan and systems. Maybe, like I did, you will even find a future business partner.

Who are the senior people or "competitors" in your market that you can reach out to for coffee or lunch?

DAY 43

Know Your Audience and Focus on It for a Year. For Real – A YEAR!

Every year there are a half dozen top conferences in the mortgage space. My company hosts two specifically for mortgage professionals, and then one a year that covers lead generation in general. (For more information see www.ConsolidatedCoaching.com.) Hundreds, sometimes thousands, of loan officers flock to Las Vegas, San Diego, Atlantic City or Los Angeles to learn from other top producers, coaches, and influencers in the mortgage industry. After every event, I see loan officers come back to the office fired up about a different lead generating strategy.

"Realtors are driving me nuts." "They are too high mainte-nance." "KW is opening their own mortgage company." "Buyers are liars." "Buyers referred by Realtors end up shopping me for a better rate." "Online lenders are killing me." These are just some of the angry comments I hear from loan officers. Directly followed by, *"I'm switching to working with other financial professionals like accountants, divorce lawyers, and estate at-*

torneys. These loan referrals will be better since they come from financial professionals."

For the record, this second statement may be true. I have friends who have built incredible careers as loan officers, life insurance salesmen, lawyers, and car insurance brokers with nothing more than referrals from other financial professionals. They appear to have a bit less stress than me. And referrals that come from other trusted advisors and financial professionals do tend to be a little stronger.

However, if you want to radically change your business and prospect to an entirely new group of people or referral sources, you CANNOT do so for a day, a week, or a month. You have to be laser-focused on this new business vertical for at least one entire year, maybe longer depending on your industry. This idea of switching referral sources, which every loan officer probably kicks around at least once a year, is appealing. However, I rarely see anyone execute on it due to the level of commitment it takes to change your lead-generation strategy and vertical.

So, why do I spend today telling you about a lead-generating technique that I DO NOT want you to use? The purpose is twofold:

1) I want you to recommit, consciously and subconsciously, to the vertical you are currently lead generating in.

2) If you are at the top of your game in one area, if you have truly saturated your market in a particular sales vertical, then I give you permission to start thinking about another vertical you can prospect. For example, a loan officer who has TRULY attempted for a year (or more) to get in front of every top Realtor in his area needs to now database 50 local CPAs and financial planners. He needs to start calling weekly, for at least one year, to try to get into a new channel of business.

Are you ready to start an additional channel of business, or do you need to recommit to the one you already have?

DAY 44

Think of Blue Ocean Strategies

Today, you will experience one of the few contradictions in this book.

Let's start with yesterday's topic. If changing the group to which you lead generate resonated with you, and if you're willing to radically change your business model by committing to lead generating to a new group of referral sources for a year, you obviously need to give it a lot of thought. One avenue is doing further research on the concept of Blue Ocean Strategies.

Blue Ocean Strategies, as outlined in the book Blue Ocean Strategies by Chan Kim, explains the process of evaluating your sector and finding your Blue Ocean. This succinctly means bypassing the *"Red Ocean Strategies,"* (AKA sailing outside of the bloody waters where everyone is killing each other over marketing and fighting for market share) and creating a new sector for your business—blue waters! This strategy has been proven to help more people earn higher profits and become a market maker instead of a *"me-too"* business professional.

DAY 44 – THINK OF BLUE OCEAN STRATEGIES

Hundreds of loan officers throughout Los Angeles are trying to land business and capture referrals from the top 200 Realtors. Maybe only a dozen loan officers are trying to capture the mortgage referrals of the top 200 divorce attorneys, estate attorneys, and business managers throughout Los Angeles. If you're looking for new waters to fish in, search for clear blue waters where the sharks aren't trying to kill each other.

Another great example that comes to mind is my friend Charles Martin who owns his own State Farm agency. The general insurance business model is to buy online leads and try to churn out as many low-cost car insurance policies as possible. It's a volume-based business with an average agency having to write between 50 and 100 policies a month to get to profitability. The thought is that car insurance buyers eventually become homeowners (with fire insurance), parents (with life insurance), and business owners (with employment policies). It's a long slog, and frankly, in Southern California where home prices are so high and business regulations make it hard to start a business, Charles was rightfully worried about this model. Furthermore, he knew that every lead he bought would also be getting five other calls from five other (cheaper priced) insurance agents.

Upon opening his office, Charles made the conscious decision to adopt a Blue Ocean Strategy and go straight for business owners and luxury car owners. By working longer, harder, and more creatively to get in front of business owners and luxury car owners, Charles was able to bypass the red oceans of low-cost, basic car insurance policies and move directly to a client base that would need all of State Farm's suite of services.

If you're 45 days into this experiment and are either A) absolutely crushing it and tapped out on people to call in your vertical OR B) completely burnt out by calling on your current pool of

referral sources and are about to give up, spend some time formu-
lating a Blue Ocean Strategy.

What group of prospects or referral sources are untapped who
could potentially fill your pipeline with quality leads?

Today, stick with what you know for at least 30 minutes. Then
spend 30 minutes brainstorming about some *"blue oceans"* you
could explore.

> *Where are there blue oceans waiting*
> *for you in your market?*

DAY 45

Let Quantity LEAD to Quality

If you're this far into the book, if you've been following my tips, if you've been putting in the time and the work, then leads should really be flowing in. At least trickling in. If your business is anything like mine, then the first few leads you get from a referral source (who will be trying you out for the first time) will not be super high-quality.

One loan officer who I helped coach from newbie to top producer tells the following story:

"You've heard of the company Build-A-Bear? For the first 2 years of my career I was known as Build-A-Buyer! I took every shitty lead with low credit, no income, and no down payment. I literally got them jobs, helped repair their credit, bought them financial books, found them co-signers, and coached them into a spot where they were financially secure enough to qualify for a home loan. Then I gave them back to the referral source and helped the referring Realtor get them into escrow."

DAY 45 – LET QUANTITY LEAD TO QUALITY

It was a lot of work, but it paid off. In 4 short years, my friend and colleague, Cole, went from earning $40,000 a year to a sustainable $200,000 a year.

Many salespeople feel like their life would be so much easier, and their business would be booming, if they could just find those magical lead sources or referral partners who are:

1) Easy to work with.

2) Do a lot of business with high-end clients.

3) Close a high percentage of the deals they refer to us.

Unfortunately, *"finding"* these kinds of perfect clients and referral partners takes time, energy, and lots and lots of contacts. You have to LEAD with quantity, talk to as many people as possible, and treat every referral and potential client with respect. Then you can whittle down the list of contacts to find those perfect partners.

Don't make the same mistake that so many people do when they meet Cole today. They assume his *"VA.Guru"* angle for helping Veterans get home loans made him an overnight success. What they don't see or know about is the quantity of leads he had to work through, many of which were low-quality at the time he received the initial lead, in order to build quality relationships.

> *Are you passing on "build-a-buyer" type leads when your business allows you the time to work on them? Are you forgetting that quantity will eventually lead to quality?*

DAY 46
Don't Pigeonhole Yourself

Down payment assistance loan programs, knows as DPA or "DAPS", are a powerful tool for home buyers across America. Some of these programs are geared toward low-to-moderate income buyers. Some are specific to revitalization projects in geographical areas. Several are simply government programs designed to increase homeownership and grow communities.

The challenge with DPA loans for lenders and loan officers is that they are traditionally difficult to process, time consuming, and designed to be on the lowest spectrum of profitability for mortgage companies. However, many loan officers grow their business, attract new referral sources, and help first-time buyers who may eventually be move-up buyers by utilizing these products. DPA loans can be a powerful tool for the loan officer trying to break into a new market or create an angle to attract new referral partners.

Unfortunately, I have observed MANY loan officers over the years who get pigeonholed by their own success with this suite of products. I've seen countless loan officers get *"stuck"* being the *"down payment assistance"* expert who Realtors never bring additional business to.

As powerful as it can be to have a niche, be careful! As you are lead generating, be conscious of how you are positioning yourself, branding yourself, and be sure you have a path to selling additional products and services.

There is nothing wrong leading with a product that might not be as profitable to you or your company. Doing the right thing for the client is always the best action you can take. However, don't forget that bad things happen to companies and salespeople who aren't profitable.

On the contrary, I also enjoyed Chris Lochhead's book *Niche Down*. Chris advocates only going for a small niche of the marketplace and dominating it.

> *Whichever direction you go, are you giving thought to how you are positioning yourself in the marketplace? Is this this niche or market position big enough and profitable enough to sustain you?*

DAY 47

Don't Be Bitchy!

If you're reading this book, I already suspect that you're not a complainer. You're not the type of person to dwell on how *"hard"* this sales job is. *"Bitchy"* can be a derogatory word used most often used toward women, OR, as it's used here, it is a derogatory word used toward sales professionals who constantly complain about the job that they have chosen for themselves.

Hopefully, you start your day expressing gratitude in a written or spoken manner. I like to use a daily journal that forces me to write down three random things that I'm grateful for. However, if for some reason you have fallen into the trap of complaining about your lead-generation activities—AKA being bitchy—I'm here to remind you that you've got it easy. You are most likely in a position where you can generate an unlimited income simply by picking up the phone, drafting an email, and lead generating.

If you think you have it hard, let me tell you about a friend I lost contact with 20 years ago when I left the U.S. Army. When I was stationed at Fort Riley, which is in the absolute middle of nowhere, I knew a guy named Blossom who was from Alabama.

He couldn't wait to get out of the Army. He wasn't well-educated, but he was very smart. Blossom was a great family guy, he was raising two kids and sending some money home to his mom. He did all this on the paltry salary of a Specialist E-4, which at the time earned about $1,850 a month.

The micromanagement of every area of our lives as infantry soldiers, the boredom of routines, the 50% of non-combat-tested leadership who scared and annoyed us all, meant he was literally counting down the days out loud once he became a double-digit-midget (meaning he had less than 99 days left in service to the Army). Although he was a good soldier and rarely complained, I suspected at the time, and still believe today, that he hated everything about the Army and couldn't want to get out and start his *"real life."*

Two days before he was free to leave, Blossom surprised us all by re-enlisting. He headed to Fort Campbell to a new unit and started working towards a promotion. We were shocked. He admitted to us that he had evaluated his options and decided that the Army, at $19,000 a year, was better than digging ditches in a dead-end job back in Alabama. I suspect Blossom has since retired from the Army and hopefully has built a great life for himself and his family on the $35,000(ish) a year he probably makes from his military pension.

If you are in a job that requires lead generation, you probably have a path to making $35,000 a MONTH. Don't take it for granted. Don't waste the opportunity that a sales job gives you. Remember that there are smart, high-quality people out there who feel that doing a job they hate, in a profession they can't stand, making in a year what you can make in a month, is worth not having to dig ditches in the Alabama heat.

Don't complain; go lead generate for an hour and build a business for you and your family.

> *Do you have a healthy perspective on your job, or are you just being bitchy?*

DAY 48

If You Don't Call, You'll Never Know

"It took me a long time to understand that when you're a salesperson, NO is a net-neutral answer."

—*Justin Bayle, 2017*

Let me explain this great quote by my friend and fellow loan officer. If you make the call, if you prospect, if you lead generate, and you get a NO, you're exactly where you were before you made the call. I un-derstand, you didn't make a sale, but you also didn't lose a sale. As a matter fact, you probably learned something while getting that no that can help you refine your strategy for your next sales call.

There are only two possible reasons that you don't make more lead generation calls: fear or ego. Fear, specifically of rejection, gets in the way; we all have fear. And pride prevents us from being willing to take that rejection; we all have an ego.

I'm here to tell you to GET OVER IT.

DAY 48 – IF YOU DON'T CALL, YOU'LL NEVER KNOW

Your ego and your fear will get you nowhere. The area where I have most experienced this is with online leads, specifically leads I frequently get from Yelp.

My fear is that if the lead is a *"good"* lead, and they found me online, that also means they found other good lenders online. I am afraid that I'll do all the work in the pre-approval stage, adding a ton of value to the deal by helping to get the offer accepted, only to get rate-shopped by this unknown, online client who will find a better deal once we are under contract. And I'll lose the commission. As you can see, it's all fear-based.

OR my ego gets in the way with the thought that this Yelp referral was an online lead who was calling around because they had been declined everywhere else. Why would I waste my time talking to this *"low-value"* client who has a low probability of making me money? See, ego.

In taking on the 60-day process of writing this book, I decided to quadruple down on my lead-generation activity and commit to generating 100 leads a month for the 2 months that I worked on this book. Clearly, I could not let fear or ego get in the way of servicing an online Yelp lead.

Lo and behold, a recent Yelp call not only turned into a $6,000 commission for my team, but it also brought an agent to the transaction who I did not have a previous relationship with. We impressed this Realtor and now have a new referral source who has the potential to bring in $100,000 of revenue for our team over the next 3-5 years.

Don't let fear or ego get in the way for the next 60 minutes. Know that NO is neutral at worst and helps you get better most of the time. Go for no and make some calls.

Is fear or ego getting in the way of allowing yourself to hear No?

AND

Do you understand that "NO" is just a neutral answer?

DAY 49

Never Stop Hunting

Here is my favorite objection. I've heard it my entire career as a loan officer when calling Realtors to try and set appointments:

"Thanks for reaching out, Scott. I've actually heard great things about you, but you know, I'm only a listing agent."

I have a hard time believing this statement, even when I know it's true! I usually hold my tongue even though what I want to say is, *"on every single real-estate transaction in America there is a seller and a buyer. You're telling me you just give up on 50% of all the available transactions and money-making opportunities in your field? Are you lying to me or are you stupid?"*

Granted, my wording is a bit different than that. Usually, the agent will come back with something along the lines of, *"I've been doing this so long that I have a nice database of clients which I farm and get listings from."* Or *"Buyers are liars, I prefer to go with the guaranteed money of having listings."* Ok, fine, I get it. Listings are a more guaranteed source of income. I also know from experience that there is real temptation, a siren call from your database that says you've made it, that tells you that you can rest on your laurels and just do listings (or for us mortgage professionals, just do refinances from our database of clients).

However, now having been in this field for 18 years, here is what normally happens to those Realtors who stop lead generating for buyers AND do not build out a team to service that side of the business. They fall off the radar in 5-7 years. Intrinsically, clients who list their home are moving out of the area about 50% of the time or are buying their last home that they will keep for 20-30 years. Effectively, as a listing agent, you may have just completed a transaction that sent your lifelong client directly out of your sphere. I cannot tell you the number of agents who were *"big deals"* in my market area 5 years ago and who are now playing catch up.

The problem is this: even if you have a great crop growing in your backyard, even if you can generate 50, 60, or even 90% of your income from your own farm—YOU STILL have to go out and hunt at least 1 hour a day. Those who don't will experience a major disruption back on the farm, a metaphorical dust-bowl of sorts, and they will have lost a lot of their hunter-gatherer skills needed to replenish their business pipeline.

Today, if you are in constant *"hunter"* mode, go tend to your own farm and work on your own crops (AKA do some lead generation within your database with past clients). Go check in with your current referral sources, pipeline of business, and closed clients.

If you have found yourself drifting toward becoming a full-time *"farmer,"* get out and hunt for some new relationships right now before it's too late.

Are you more of a "hunter" or a "farmer" at this point in your business? Which area do you need to give some attention to?

DAY 50

The Danger of Being BUSY and NOT PRODUCTIVE

Yesterday, were you busy or were you productive?

Today, do you have a WRITTEN plan, calendar reminders, a guide for the day, and/or an accountability partner to ensure you stay productive and not just busy?

In your career, have you maximized your time, effort, and opportunity by staying productive and not just busy?

Here is a classic example. You're at your desk when an email comes in that is addressed to several parties in your organization, and you are CC'd on the correspondence. This email has something to do with you, your client, the sales process, or closing a deal. Maybe it's something that you feel needs to be triaged immediately in order to keep your pipeline full and to put money in your pocket.

You are CC'd on the email so technically there is probably someone else in the *"To:"* field who should be handling this particular email, but you jump in anyway. Several emails, 2 miscommunications with requests for clarifications, and a few obligatory thank yous later, problem solved and you move on with your day, feeling good that you spent 30 minutes *"solving the problem"* addressed in this email. The reality is you jumped in when you probably didn't need to just so you could act busy.

It is now the very next day and the same scenario occurs, but instead of being at your desk doing busy work, you are at lunch with a prospective client being productive and asking for additional referrals. You get back to your car and check your email. You see a 13-message email exchange between Bill in marketing and Suzy in accounting with a bunch of people CC'd (yourself included). Without you being involved, the problem gets solved (or nearly solved with you only needing to give a quick approval, reply, or confirmation). This takes 2 minutes out of your day and you move on to the next sales appointment.

In which scenario were you busy, and in which scenario were you productive? Now, extrapolate this hypothetical exercise out over the course of a week, a month, a year, or even a career! How much time have you wasted being busy instead of productive?

And look, I get it. We live in an age where clients and referral partners have an expectation of immediate response, gratification, and access to information. Thanks to Amazon, our endless supply of *"on-demand"* access to products and services, and the *"one-click"* society we live in, has set us up for failure in the business world (especially for those of us who work in businesses or sales processes with complex steps). However, YOU must have a plan, a system, or a team for addressing these client needs without getting sucked into the endless busy work. You must stay productive at least 50% of the time to have any shot at being a top producer in your field.

Today, I challenge you to STAY productive and eliminate at least 10 items on your plate or in your inbox that you know are just busy work. Send someone else out to grab lunch; they fly, you buy. Let a few email chains resolve themselves without you jumping in. Turn off 90% of the automatic notifications on your phone that create distractions and busy work. Stay productive and go lead generate for an hour.

What are the busywork tasks that can be resolved without you today?

DAY 51

Know Your Enemy (or Competitor)

Eric is a top-producing loan officer who has built his business in a much different way than me. Eric gets 90% of his loans and most of his clients from two unique sources: CPAs and his competitors.

Eric works for a mortgage banker who might not have the best rates, but has access to dozens of products for clients whose financial situations fall slightly outside the box of traditional bank lenders. He leverages these products and his deep understanding of income structures and tax returns to educate his clients, his referral sources, AND his competitors.

I know my guidelines. I work at a company where they have insane resources geared toward helping me and my team structure loans, build loans, and find guidelines that help clients qualify for home loans. However, if I want to know what Bank of America, Citibank, or Wells Fargo's guidelines are, I call Eric. He knows, almost by memory, what each of his competitors can and cannot do.

DAY 51 – KNOW YOUR ENEMY (OR COMPETITOR)

When he gets a client who is rate-sensitive and who is thinking of going with their bank, Eric knows exactly why (or why not) that client will (or will not) be approved for a loan with that bank. If the client won't qualify, Eric educates his client about the challenges of starting the loan process over with Wells, BofA, Chase, or some other large financial institution. If the client WILL qualify at another bank, and Eric is going to lose the deal anyway, he directly refers the client to a competing loan officer who he knows and trust at that particular bank.

His hope is that when that bank loan officer runs across a deal he cannot do, or a tax return he cannot interrupt, then Eric is going to be the first call to get that loan.

Furthermore, proactively handing off a client and doing what's *"best"* for the consumer is one of the fastest ways Eric builds trust with his original referral sources, who tend to be CPAs, investment specialist, and money managers who the buyer already uses.

Knowing the guidelines that affect your product and service is key to being a competent sales professional. Knowing your competitors' guidelines can turn you into a world class producer.

Today, I want you to spend half of your time lead generating, as you normally would, with your standard pool of referral sources. However, I also want you to spend a half-hour doing some research on your competition. See which one of your competitors you can get out to coffee or lunch to understand what they do better and what they do worse than you and your company. You might find a new referral source in a competitor who can actually send you deals.

Which "competitors" can you contact today and work toward turning into referral partners?

DAY 52

There Are No "Part-Time" Salespeople

I'm not a great poker player. When I'm opinionated (and I'm very opinionated on a lot of topics, I cannot help but visually express my disgust or approval on that topic), I wear my emotions on my sleeve, and I'm pretty easy to read.

My business partner and my team usually know what kind of mood I'm in within 2 seconds of seeing me in the morning. Sorry. It's something I'm working on. Because of this, I'm sure a lot of people have seen my disgust when they tell me about being a *"part-time this or that."*

It's my belief that you cannot be a *"part-time"* anything. You can have passion projects. You can work two 40-hours a week jobs and do each full-time. You can have hobbies. However, I strongly believe in Malcolm Gladwell's thesis that he laid out in his book Outliers. Gladwell states that in order to TRULY master a craft, you must practice it for 10,000 hours.

DAY 52 - THERE ARE NO "PART-TIME" SALESPEOPLE

The best example in Outliers is the story of The Beatles. They weren't some random, overnight success story. Instead, they were a group of young, hard-working, 20-year-old British kids who had practiced together and played the German underground club scene as teens until they amassed 10,000 hours of expertise as musicians. By the time they hit the U.S. and started recording albums, they were already seasoned pros.

Similarly, I have a friend who wanted to make as much mindless money as possible over the course of 2-3 years so he could have the capital to build a new business. For nearly 3 years he drove Uber 12-16 hours a day, 7 days a week, 52 weeks a year. By the time he saved enough money to move on from driving (not coincidentally by putting in almost 10,000 hours), he knew every hustle in the book. He knew how to sign up drivers for a $300 referral fee, what routes and pick-up locations were most profitable, how to rent out his car to other Uber drivers while he was sleeping, and how to record data from his dashboard and sell it back to self-driving startup companies.

By going all-in on one job, even if it wasn't his passion, he became an expert at that particular hustle. His record, while trying to raise $20,000 to attend a week-long training in Scotland, was $21,000 in just 12 days (between his Uber driving and his car rental service). My point is that my friend could not have accomplished this by part-timing it or doing a half-assed job. By going all-in and obtaining 10,000 hours of experience, even at something as trivial as driving Uber, my friend was able to set himself up for the next stage of his career.

Are you a full-time sale professional that is actually half-assing and part-timing your Lead generation? The sales industry is full of people who want to start part-time, never fully commit, or show up 40+ hours a week but only put in 5 hours of quality work. Don't be that guy. Commit to your Lead Generation activities and watch your pipeline fill up.

> *Are you fully committed to your craft, or are you trying to get away with "part-timing" it? How can you spend more quality hours Lead generating?*

DAY 53

Work/Life Balance Is an Illusion

Three things happened on the day I was writing this chapter. In what you could call coincidence or fate, the following occurred:

1) This was one of the 8 chapters I outlined a month ago and planned to write today.

2) One of my coaching clients sent me an email asking about work/life balance, and I posted a video response in our private coaching Facebook group. In general, she was wondering how I juggle so many balls—loan origination, management, coaching, family, writing a book, etc.

3) As I write this, I'm currently locked in a hotel room in Huntington Beach, totally ignoring my family and business for the weekend, while I finish this book. No work/life balance here whatsoever! I'm all-in on finishing this book.

I'm here to tell you that work/life balance is a myth created by gurus who don't know any better. That businessman you follow on Facebook who makes all the right moves might currently be, or has been, millions of dollars in debt and/or has declared bankruptcy. That spiritual leader or perfect family man (or woman) you follow on Facebook who completely shocked you when he (or she) announced a pending divorce... Yeah, that person was cheating.

That 55-year-old Ironman you work with who has a body to be envied and a bank account you would kill for, might have a son who hates him for never being home on the weekends. That super nice guy at church who always seems to be doing something for the community, he could be in AA and only have found community service after his second DUI. That mentor you look up to who survives on 3 hours of sleep a night and seems to complete huge projects at will, he had cancer and almost died because he never gave his body a rest.

Anyone who claims to have it all figured out is either lying to you, or they are delusional and lying to themselves. Most likely, you are reading too much into their social media persona because EVERYONE has their baggage, their demons, their flaws. It's our job as members of society to know what our baggage is, what's in our suitcase and deal with it as best we can.

The greatest athletes in the world, the titans of business, the top producers at your company, the leaders of your church—it's highly UNLIKELY that they are balanced. I mean seriously, what does that even mean? Eight hours at work, 7.25 hours sleeping, 0.75 hours cuddling the spouse or the dog, 4 hours with kids, 2 hours on personal development, 2 hours on fun... come on! The term work/life balance makes no sense to begin with unless you define it for yourself, which is hard to do when everyone is trying to define it for you.

When I want to accomplish something, I specifically take myself OUT of balance and go all-in. That's what you should be doing with lead generation. Go all-in for one hour a day for the rest of your life -OR- in 61-day *"burns"* as outlined in this book. Don't let anyone else define what you should be doing during that hour. If you are truly committed to accomplishing your goals, then know that one hour of lead generation is going to be part of your ethos from here on out.

The good news is that there's a solution for this work/life balance dilemma. You can commit to being PRESENT. Use meditation, read a book on the topic, get private coaching from Julianna Raye (she's the best), OR just turn off your FUCKING CELL PHONE. (I almost did it, I almost got to the end of the book without using the F word).

Seriously, it's that important; it's that impactful. In this crazy, overly connected, overwhelming society we live in, being present is just about the most important thing you can do for yourself and for others who you care about.

If you find yourself out of balance with yourself, your psyche, your spouse, your kids, your friends, TURN OFF YOUR cell phone and be present. It's the secret weapon I use to combat the constant distraction that our cell phones have become. Trust me, try it for 30-60 minutes every day, and it will change your life.

Many days I only get 20 quality minutes with my son, daughter, or wife before life takes over, baths have to be drawn, and bills have to be paid. An uninterrupted cigar with a friend is a rare treat. A private conversation with my best friend, in person, happens about once a year. The only way I can make these moments count is by eliminating distractions, being present, and focusing on the person (or the task) that is right in front of me. Work on being present with the people who count the most (including yourself). That way you can focus on being present, guilt-free, with your business and with lead generation as needed!

DAY 53 – WORK/LIFE BALANCE IS AN ILLUSION

Have you given up on the work/life balance myth and committed to being present?

OR

More importantly, what does "balance" and being "present" look like to you?

DAY 54
Think Big – REALLY Big

In 2014, I went to Hal Elrod's Best Year Ever Blueprint event (a must attend event every December, BTW). One of my business associates was going through a nasty divorce, feeling down, and needed a kick-start going into 2015. I happened to have listened to The Miracle Morning as it was the $1.99 *"book deal of the day"* on Audible and I was impressed with Hal's optimism. My buddy and I trekked down to San Diego and decided we were going to participate without any judgment. I'll be honest, it was hard...very hard.

There was singing and dancing. A DJ and an aerobic instructor who pumped us up in between breaks. Some guy named *"Brotha James"* was beating a drum. There was even a mindfulness exercise with some hippie who had us close our eyes. It was all outside of my comfort zone. WAY outside of my comfort zone. (Sidenote: I have since become friends with all of these people.)

By the time lunch rolled around on Day 1 of this two-day event, I was almost ready to bail. We decided to stay through the after-lunch keynote speaker and then make our decision. The next 3 hours, I can say with all honesty, changed my life.

Two things happened. I experienced, yes, experienced, Jon Vroman's speech on living life in the front row. I was also led through a 10x exercise by Hal's partner-in-crime, Jon Berghoff. The 10x method is an exercise where you write down certain goals, and then work on a plan that helps you imagine and achieve that goal at a factor of 10 times the originally stated goal.

Jon Vroman's speech is something you must see at some point in your life. It will force you to reflect on how you are living your life and encourage you to take more chances and have more "Front-Row" moments. It was this speech, coupled with the 10x exercise led by Jon Berghoff and Hal Elrod, that was the real eye-opener for me and contributed greatly to improving my life over the following 12 months.

After writing down a handful of personal and professional goals, Jon and Hal had us journal for nearly half an hour on all the things we needed to do in order to 10x that goal. As I wanted to make $300,000 that following year, I was forced to brainstorm on what I would need to do, what I would need to learn, who I would need to become, who I would need to surround myself with in order to make $3,000,000. The task of writing down everything I could do to 10x my goal was scary, enlightening, and empowering.

I wanted to also drop 10 lbs. What would I have to do in order to go from slightly healthier to triathlete?

I wanted to have some success in the dating arena? That wasn't enough, 10x it. What would it look like to be happily married with a great family? What were all the areas of my life I could improve upon at a factor of 10 so that I could dramatically affect myself, the people around me, and the world?

The point is not that I made (or have YET to make $3M in a year). I haven't completed an Ironman just yet. However, the exercise of thinking big caused me to open my mind to new possibilities, new solutions, and new systems that could help me dramatically change the direction of my life.

In 2015, I more than doubled my income, married a wonderful woman named Karina, opened a coaching business, and deepened key friendships that will remain for a lifetime.

As you near the end of this 61-day Challenge on Lead Generation, you may be feeling some new sense of personal satisfaction, coupled with an expanding desire for new business and personal successes. Now that you know that you are 100% in control of your financial future, I want you to spend some time thinking about how you can do more. I continue to challenge you by recommending that you take 30 minutes, today over your lunch, to work through this 10x exercise.

Spend some time brainstorming about what's next. How can you go bigger in your business and your life? Whether you've gen-erated one qualified lead or 100 qualified leads in the last 2 months, what would need to happen to 10x that number? Who would you have to hire? Who would you need to become to handle this vol-ume of business? What training would you need? What systems would you need to put into place?

I promise you that completing this journaling exercise can change your life as it did for me. Now go lead generate. Then spend your lunch journal writing about your goals at a 10x level.

What would your life look like if you attempted to 10X your goals?

DAY 55

Write It Down

Yesterday, I talked about the power of how one single journaling exercise dramatically changed my life. There is power in writing stuff down. Freeflow journaling exercises, daily planners designed to help hold you accountable (right now I use the Panda Planner activity journal), even keeping an old-school checklist, can all dramatically help increase your retention and productivity.

I have volumes of notebooks filled with personal goals, notes from conferences and seminars I've attended, lists of business ideas, takeaways from masterminds groups I've participated in, and the list goes on and on. Frequently, I never even review these notes. However, just the act of writing them down makes it more real, helps me retain the information, and somehow propels me into action in a way that digital note-taking just can't replicate.

Millions of people have found that a shift back to written journals and planners can be helpful. We humans find huge value from taking 5 minutes a day (or at night) to organize our thoughts, our schedules, and write down our ideas using pen and paper.

DAY 55 - WRITE IT DOWN

As we near the end of our 61-day journey, you may have lots of scattered thoughts you want to get down on paper. You might need to develop a written system of accountability to keep the momentum of lead generation moving forward. You might have found that tracking your daily leads on paper and then moving to a digital platform each night, or once a week, works best for you.

Whatever the goal or the reason, I highly recommend you try writing more stuff down for the next 30 days. You may find this helps with your retention and follow-through.

What tool will you use to Write It Down?

AND

How can journaling help you stick to your lead generation practice even after you're done with this book?

DAY 56

Ideas Are Cool – Action Creates Greatness

Hope is not a plan. The business world (and life) appears to me to be divided into two groups of people: doers and thinkers.

In a society as complex as ours, it's important to have thinkers; it's important to have academics. We need people who spend large amounts of their time thinking about what could be.

However, in sales there are no excuses. Planning is needed. Reflecting is important. Revising your technique for better efficiencies and learning more skills are necessary aspects to growing your business. HOWEVER, if you are in a job that requires lead generation as a core means of production, then you must lean heavily toward being a doer. And you must do things over and over again to start the snowball of success.

I see it on social media all the time—loan officers who bias towards being thinkers instead of doers. They are great at strategizing, talking, posting on social media, presenting a facade of success. Sometimes they know rates, guidelines, and understand market forces at a deeper level than I ever will. Then I look up their funding numbers (which has become public knowledge in the loan business), or I interview them for employment and review their W2 from the previous year, and I see that they are failing in their careers.

Inevitably, when I run across this type of person in my interviews to hire new loan officers, I often ask the following question, *"How much time in a day do you spend lead generating?"* I'm inevitably met with a blank stare. This is when I know I'm interviewing a thinker and not a doer.

People with cool ideas can occasionally become famous for their deep thoughts. Conversely, people who take action have a much greater possibility of creating opportunities for themselves, their families, their community, and are frequently the ones who actually change the world.

Don't be a thinker. Don't look at your pad of paper, your spreadsheet, your call list, or your lead sheets and overthink what calls you're going to make or how you are going to make them. Just pick up the phone and do the 1 hour of lead-generation activities that you KNOW you need to accomplish.

What action can you take today to move from being a thinker to a doer?

DAY 57

That Which Can Be Measured Can Be Improved

Look at your lead tracking spreadsheet or Google Sheet, which you BETTER have started on Day 2 as I directed. What are you seeing? Which trends are being established? What patterns are emerging? Which referral sources are actually providing leads? Which referral sources are you tempted to cut off because their leads always seem to be time-wasters and are not going to become real deals.

Have you been able to track, over the course of the last 2 months, an increase in the volume of your leads received? If not, please email me at Scott@ScottGrovesTeam.com for a full refund.

Do you have so many new leads that are going to convert to closed business that it's time to go to management and start talking about hiring support staff ahead of demand?

Prior to buying a billion dollars of suspect loans on the second-ary market, Washington Mutual, my former employer, was actually a very well-run company. WaMu strongly believed in the corporate philosophy of *"What can be measured can be improved."* At times, as a branch level employee, it was annoying that I had to spend 10-15 minutes each day *"tracking"* my results. Wasn't this just 10-15 minutes stolen from me when I could be making a sale? Wasn't this just wasted data that management ignored?

What I've learned as my career has progressed and I've started to manage more people, is that I was absolutely mistaken in my understanding of the importance of tracking. Used correctly, as we are doing with our leads, tracking is an invaluable tool. Knowing where your leads are coming from, when they are coming in, and having contact information for everyone who enters your sphere is an amazing tool.

Furthermore, you will soon be able to use your tracking to advocate for more resources and possibly higher pay.

Additionally, being able to quickly upload your database to various platforms is also a powerful tool. I want you to have a digital copy of your book of business, correct contact information for referral sources and clients, and a database that you can quickly use when a new digital tool presents itself. Keeping an accurate spreadsheet will save you hundreds of hours of data entry when your industry inevitably moves to a new platform or sales tool.

Today, as you lead generate, be sure you are tracking your leads on a daily basis.

What are 2-3 ways you can see using your database as a tool to evaluate business trends and opportunities?

DAY 58

Look for Chaos and Be Excited for the Hard Times

"Make it harder. Make it Harder. Make it Harder." Over my career as a mortgage loan officer, I've heard this motto from top-producing loan officers, managers, and seasoned veterans of the sales community.

You should embrace this same motto as a Lead Generator. When things get hard, people quit.

When there is chaos in the marketplace, when there is blood in the streets (financially), people quit.

When government regulations, disruptive technologies, or natural disasters make it harder to earn a living in a particular industry, people quit.

When business gets harder, lazy salespeople take the path of least resistance, find new jobs, transfer into support roles, take *"time-off"* for new opportunities, go on unemployment, or change industries.

But guess what? Those who commit to a daily practice of lead generation, those who survive will come out on the other side of the turmoil with more market share and will thrive.

Following the financial crisis of 2009, my industry saw plummeting property values, political turmoil, slow markets, government intervention, and tougher guidelines. There was a mass exodus of loan officers and Realtors who were able to make a good living leading up to the crash, but didn't have the chops, the lead-generation skills, the client base, or the savings to weather the storm and stay in the business.

In the last 2 months, if you've made it this far, I'm sure there have absolutely been some hard times. Maybe you've even seen some changes in your industry in the short time you've been following along in this book. EMBRACE the change, get excited about harder times ahead, and know that by consistently lead generating and growing your pipeline, you can make it in any market. Today, think of a challenge you've overcome in your career or industry and use this as a talking point during today's lead-generation calls. Use your success and ability to overcome previous adversity as the fuel to lead generate every single day.

> *What is a recent challenge you overcame that made you a better person as a result? Are you ready for the next disruption in your industry?*

DAY 59

Rinse and Repeat – AGAIN

This page isn't an error from the printer or a mistake by my book editor.

Trust me, I haven't run out of ideas for lead generating and capturing new business. A majority of the time that you spend lead generating, I want you to focus on contacting new and existing referral sources who can fill your pipeline. However, following up with your existing leads and past clients is paramount to not having to reinvent the wheel each day or in each new sales cycle.

How often you follow up with your existing leads is SO IMPORTANT that it's getting several pages in this short book. You've made it; you made it a FULL two months. Today is a day for follow-up with the top 25 people you've talked to, connected with, or wish you had connected with in the last 60 days. So many sales professionals are willing to make the first call to a prospect, potential lead, or referral source. Maybe they even make the second call; however, it's these third, fourth, and fifth calls that ACTUALLY win the day.

DAY 59 – RINSE AND REPEAT – AGAIN

Today, do NOT focus generating new leads or contacting new referral sources. Spend an hour reaching out to important referral sources or clients you've come across over the last two months.

> *Who are the prospects that have said no, who you can call again today? What past client do you need to get in touch with today just to say, Hi? What potential client is sitting in your spreadsheet or Google Doc who you haven't connected with and need to try again today?*

DAY 60

It's Almost Over, Now It's Time for the Hard Stuff

If you're doing, or have done, any significant amount of business over your career, or maybe even over the last 60 days, then you've inevitably fouled up a deal. At some point, you've forgotten to get back to someone or dropped the ball with at least one potential client or referral source. Chances are you can think of a few deals where you royally screwed up.

I'm here to tell you it's OK. Although we always want to be refining our systems, improving our sales process, and adding value to our clients and referral sources, we are still going to screw something up. No matter how successful we become, we are only human. We are going to make mistakes.

The best thing you can do is reach out to the people involved in these failures and talk to them anyway. Apologize, take personal responsibility, or maybe get really uncomfortable and perform a self-accusation audit (google it—it's a concept pioneered by Chris Voss in his book Never Split the Difference—a must read book if you lead generate for a living). Effectively, in a self-audit you diffuse the situation and disarm the discomfort of the mistake by falling on your sword and leading with all of the things you may have done wrong (both real AND perceived).

I can guarantee you it's NEVER as bad as you think it is. I recently did an accusation audit with a Realtor who I had botched 2 deals with. I fell on my sword, emailed her a list of everything I thought I might have done wrong, and then called her to review my shortcomings. I was elated to find out that she hadn't thought twice about the mistake once we had moved past it. That call led to a repaired relationship. Although I don't get deals from her directly (for now), she has been instrumental in assisting me in earning other business by endorsing me as a straight shooter to other referral sources.

If you've stuck around this long, you're tougher than you know. Make those tough calls today. It will NOT be as bad as you think.

> *Are there past failures you need to address with a self-audit and an uncomfortable phone call? Who can you call today who was party to a failed business transaction? How can you begin to repair a strained business relationship with a single, genuine phone call?*

DAY 61

Celebrate with a Follow-up Call

CELEBRATE! Give yourself some credit. Express public gratitude to anyone who has helped you along this journey. Tear up those checks you wrote two months ago!

Today is a day to go deeper with the top relationships you've built over the last 60 days. If you've put in the work, if you've made the follow-up calls, if you've been tracking your leads, you should have at least 10 relationships, referral sources, or contacts that you're proud of. Call those people again today. Check in, go deeper, and invite them out for an in-person meeting. Breaking bread with a referral source or valued client can be worth a hundred times the cost of that meal.

Your lead generation calls today should be about deepening the key relationships you've established over the last couple months.

As a parting thought, I ask you to do several things:

1) **Refer this book to a coworker or buy a copy for someone who needs it.** Who in your world could change their life by

spending an hour a day focusing on lead generation? Help that person out with a copy of this book.

2) **Since Lead Generation never ends, and we all need a kick-start from time to time, I want you to set a calendar reminder for 60 days from now to re-read this book and start over with another 61-day commitment.** That's probably about the time your commitment to lead generation will start to wane. Presumably, the work you've put in over the last 2-3 months will start to payoff with new deals. You might fall into the trap of getting stuck working IN your business (on the actual deals) versus working ON your business (AKA lead generating).

3) **To give yourself the best chance of committing to lead generation, I want you to set a recurring calendar reminder for every Monday.** Put this reminder on your business calendar, your personal calendar, and the calendars of anyone on your team. In the body of this calendar reminder, you should add your current list of top 10 matured referral sources, top 10 growing relationships, top 10 dream relationships. Ensuring you are at least reaching out to these 30 individuals every week will help you stay on track.

4) **Shortly, if it's not already available, you will be able to buy a 61-Day Lead Generation journal.** This journal will allow you to complete this challenge 2 more times, track your progress, and get additional tips, tactics, and resources.

5) **Please leave me a review on Amazon.** Honest 4 and 5 star reviews help me to sell more books. If you don't feel the book warrants a 4 or 5 star review - email at Scott@ ConsolidatedCoaching.com and I will send you a full refund.

Lastly, who can you refer *"61 Days of Lead Generation"* to in your network? Referring this book to someone else might help you to find an accountability partner, coworker, or manager who will help keep you on track.

If you're like me, you probably bought this book because you needed a jump start. I hope you got the kick in the behind that you needed. If you made it this far, actually read the material, and more importantly, followed the steps, then you've completed a 2-month journey that only 5% of readers will commit to.

It's been said that it takes between 30 and 61 days to develop a DAILY habit, but it only takes roughly 3-7 days to break one. If you want to continue on this journey, I highly recommend you create an event RIGHT NOW in your calendar that will remind you to do these daily activities. Refer back to this book, come find me at www.ConsolidatedCoaching.com for additional resources, reach out to me at Scott@ScottGrovesTeam.com for additional motivation, or subscribe to our YouTube channel at www.YouTube. com/ConsolidatedCoaching.

If you're a bit burnt out on daily lead generation, or if you've generated so many leads that you now need to solidify your base and nurture these leads, I get it. I give you permission to take a week off, briefly take your foot off the gas. Just be sure that you spend the hour you've already put aside for lead generation on some other growth activity. Don't get sucked into busy work! Be productive during this hour and work on developing a new, healthy habit. Read an hour a day during your week off so you can finish that book on sales and conversion you've been meaning to get to. Spend that hour a day focusing on your mental or physical health. Breaks, variety, and scheduled times of renewal are important.

HOWEVER, to continue to build your pipeline, nurture your referral sources, and grow your business, you must continue to commit to lead generation. If you're taking a week off, that's fine. The deal we have to make with each other is that you will restart this 61-day series no later than 2 weeks from today. Commit to it publicly.

I would be honored if we stayed in touch. I thank you for getting to the end of a book that took me months to write and required 18 years of experience to create.

---

www.ConsolidatedCoaching.com
www.YouTube.com/ConsolidatedCoaching
www.ConsolidatedCoaching.com/Resources
Scott@ScottGrovesTeam.com

A THANK YOU TO EVERYONE WHO HELPED

In some special way, the following people inspired me, motivated me, or were directly responsible for my business success, my personal development, and/or completion of this book.

Kirk Gerou & Eugene Ridenour - Attending that fateful wedding together in Belize, and meeting the two of you, helped me refocus my life, discover the power of lead generations, and led to opportunities that kept me employed during the tough years. I wouldn't be the professional I am today if it wasn't for your friendship and trust in me personally and professionally.

Dad & Mom - Your work ethic proved to be one of the most valuable gifts you could have imparted to your son. I appreciate you both for teaching me that hard work is always enough to get through any of the hard times that life can throw at us.

Steven Levine - Your friendships, mentorship, and willingness to proofread an endless number of emails, blog posts, and sample chapters helped give me the confidence that I need to write a book.

Justin Bayle & Karina Del Toro Groves (my partner at work and my partner at home) - Without your support this book never gets completed, our business isn't thriving as it today, and I wouldn't be the manager, father, & coach that I'm growing into. Thank you for everything you do to ensure success at home, at the office, and with my passion projects.

Jon Berghoff, Jon Vroman, Julianna Raye, "Brotha" James, & Hal Elrod - Your inaugural Best Year Ever Blueprint and the subsequent conversations we've had since that event has changed my life. It's that simple yet that impactful. I'm excited to call you all mentors and friends.

Simon Herrera, Arash Gezerseh, & Charles Martin - Your friendship, commitment to helping me manage my health (while still joining me for an occasional cigar or a glass wine), and our business conversations have been, and will continue to be some of the highlights from my adult years.

Jay Papasan, Paul Morris, David Osborn, John Ruhlin, Mike Dillard, Tucker Max, Jocko Willink, Todd Duncan - Whether you knew it or not, at some point in the last 10 years, we had a conversation that inspired me, motivated me, or encouraged me to take *Extreme Ownership* of this goal and get this book done. Thank you for your mentorship, or that call you were willing to jump on with an unproven author, and/or that quick 5-minute conversation on the way out to the parking lot after that seminar, where you, unknowingly, dropped some important knowledge into my mind. You helped make this book a reality in ways you didn't even know.

Mike Merriam, Christopher DeRosa, Steve Shull, Jeff Uniack, Robert Salazar, Henry Gonzalez, Virginia Martinez, Chad Coester, Clay Duncan, Tony

Taveekanjana, Casey Crawford, Eli Fairfield, Sam Ellsworth, Cole Strange, Ron Sequeira, Justin Grable, Al Sed, Mike Ullmann, Mike Eaton, Russell Kesterson, Josh Painter, Mark Walker, Ernest Hernandez, Mario Mazzamuto, Thomas Bayles, Natalie Salins, Stephanie Barbosa, Natalie Fornelli, Larisa Lutes, Patrick O'Driscoll, Karen Ross, Patrick Larkin, & Jessica Malen - This group, along with so many others, have been instrumental in my development as a Coach, Manager, Loan Officer, Business Professional, and as a Man. The good, the bad, the ugly. The accountability, the coaching, the mentorship, the conversations, the fights, the late night cigars, the vulnerability, the frustrations, and the successes - you have all helped me, in your own special way, to become a better person.

Chandler Bolt, Rachel McCracken, Qat Wanders - Without you three, this book never gets done. You three gave me the program, accountability, and professional support I needed to finish this book.

The Dirty Dozen - Our text message threads from the last three years has kept me going through times of challenge, disinterest, and frustration. You guys make me laugh (often), cry (sometimes - usually about politics), and always have my back as we move through these crazy times in the mortgage industry.

ABOUT THE AUTHOR

Author, Business Coach, and Top Producing Loan Officer Scott Groves has been providing quality mortgage products to his clients on the Eastside of Los Angeles for over 18 years. By fostering close relationships with real-estate agents, buyers, and sellers, Scott has built a career by consistently lead generating and providing exceptional service from application to closing.

As a business and lead generation expert, his knowledge in the fields of management, mortgage lending, coaching, and leadership has come through formal education, professional licensing, on-the-job training, and customer interaction. Scott has coached hundreds of loan officers who have followed his helpful advice and found their own pathways to success through focused lead generation.

Scott lives in Southern California. When he's not in the office or generating leads, Scott spends his free time boxing, hiking through the beautiful foothills of California with his son Gabriel, playing with his daughter Alina, or catching Hollywood's newest release with his son Jonathan or his wife Karina. An avid reader and Audible.com junkie, Scott enjoys using his book knowledge and business skills to give back to his community.